HELPING THE TEACHER

Findley B. Edge

Helping
the
Teacher

BROADMAN PRESS *Nashville, Tennessee*

To
MY MOTHER
my first and best teacher

Contents

Preface vii

Unit I

Helping the Teacher Plan a Lesson

1. *Toward Teacher Improvement*   3
   Areas in which teachers need help—Various approaches
   to teacher-training—A continuous school—The teaching
   improvement period—Advantages

2. *Steps in Preparing a Lesson*   17
   The importance of planning—Practical aids—Background
   preparation—A lesson plan outline—Selecting aims—
   Quarterly aims—Unit aims—Lesson aims—Guidance in
   lesson preparation

3. *Teaching for Conduct Response*   33
   Securing purposeful Bible study—Developing the lesson—
   Making the lesson personal—Securing carry-over—Guid-
   ance in lesson preparation

4. *Teaching to Increase Knowledge*   49
   Findings of a Bible knowledge test—Teaching with a
   knowledge aim—Factors involved in teaching knowledge
   —Steps in planning a lessson—A lesson plan—The place
   of review—The place of drill—Guidance in lesson preparation

Unit II

Helping the Teacher Use a Variety of Methods

5. *Introduction to Method*   69
   Concern about method—The broader problem of method
   —Choosing a method—Variety of method

6. *Question and Answer Method* 76
   Types of questions—Stimulating thought—Improving questions—Pupil questions—Guidance in lesson preparation

7. *The Discussion Method* 86
   The discussion method—Factors involved in a good discussion—Types of discussion—The teacher's function—Values—Limitations—Guidance in lesson preparation—Evaluating the discussion method

8. *The Lecture Method* 104
   Values—Limitations—Frequent use—Preparing the lecture—Presenting the lecture—Lecturing with profit—Guidance in lesson preparation

9. *The Story or Illustration* 117
   Relationship to learning—Purposes or uses—Sources—Using illustrations in a lesson plan—Telling the story—Qualities of a good story—Guidance in lesson preparation

10. *Role Playing* 128
    Definition—An example—Role playing in the total lesson plan—Steps in using role playing—Values and limitations—Guidance in lesson preparation

11. *The Project* 139
    The project and learning—Types—Steps in guiding a project—Values—Cautions—Guidance in lesson preparation

12. *Nonprojected Visual Aids* 150
    Chalkboard—Maps—Flat pictures—Field trips—Bulletin board—Objects—Models—Charts—Graphs—Drama—Guidance in lesson preparation

13. *Projected Visual Aids* 167
    The problem of verbalism—Principles of utilization—Motion films—Filmstrips—Slides—Opaque projection—Guidance in lesson preparation

Preface

THE MEN AND WOMEN WHO TEACH in Sunday schools are a dedicated, devoted group of people. They give freely of their time and of themselves to the task of teaching the Bible. Their teaching has blessed the lives of countless thousands. They know the spiritual importance of teaching. Yet these teachers are keenly aware of their own limitations. They want to become better teachers.

This book attempts to provide help for teachers through a better understanding of the use of the weekly officers and teachers' meeting. It is the author's thesis that the weekly officers and teachers' meeting ought to be a continuous school for teacher improvement. This book, therefore, is written as resource material to be used by a department superintendent with his teachers. Chapter 1 explains in detail the approach to be taken by the department superintendent. This is followed by a discussion of eleven teaching techniques with which teachers ought to be familiar and which they ought to use. The department superintendent should use the first part of the teaching improvement period (from eight to twenty minutes, depending whether the group has a half hour or an hour for this period) to teach the use of one of these techniques to the teachers. Several Wednesday nights may be needed to cover some techniques.

During the rest of the teaching improvement period the superintendent will lead the teachers to prepare the lesson they are to teach next Sunday, using the principle they have just studied. The superintendent must be sure to save adequate time for this lesson preparation by the teachers. The application of these principles to the lesson preparation is most important. The study of teaching principles as theory without making practical use of them has in the past been a major weakness in the training of teachers.

The book has been made as practical as possible. Topics included were selected because they are immediately applicable to the teaching of the lesson. Each discussion of teaching techniques has been carefully outlined and material included which the superintendent can use in teaching his teachers. In addition, suggestions for the superintendent to use as he guides the teachers in applying teaching techniques in lesson preparation are made.

Department superintendents are urged not to follow slavishly the materials in this book in teaching the teachers. That is exactly what teachers need to get away from in their lesson preparation and teaching. The superintendent should take this material, study it, understand it, digest it, and make it his own before he tries to teach it. He should adapt, change, leave out, and add to each topic as he seeks to meet the particular needs of his particular group of teachers.

The order in which the lessons are to be taught should be determined by the department superintendent and the teachers. It is not at all necessary to follow the order given in the book. However, the superintendent should plan ahead and make sure that the topic or educational technique to be studied on a given Wednesday night is applicable to and usable with the Sunday school lesson which the teachers will be studying that Wednesday night.

The superintendent will find that most of the topics cannot be covered in one teaching session if all the material is used. This is not necessarily a disadvantage. Let one topic serve as the basis for study for two or more Wednesday night sessions. This will give the teachers an opportunity to "practice" the principle for several Sundays in their teaching. It is not the purpose of the teaching improvement period to see how *many* topics can be covered in a given period of time. The purpose is to help the teachers *understand* and *master* the principles that are discussed, however few or many they may be. The teachers' meetings will continue week after week, indefinitely. The superintendent will have ample time to cover all the principles he desires. Both the superintendent and the teachers should take time to master the principles as they go along.

The material in this book is not new. However, an attempt has been made to present familiar principles and insights in a fresh and practical manner and to make it easier for the superintendent to share them with his teachers. This book will also prove valuable to pastors, ministers of education, and general Sunday school superintendents, as well as anyone else who has responsibility for teacher-training. Individual teachers also will find help as they make a private study of principles discussed herein and apply them in the preparation of lessons for teaching.

I would like to express my appreciation to my colleagues— Dr. Allen W. Graves, Dean of the School of Religious Education; Dr. Sabin P. Landry; Professor Ernest J. Loessner; and Professor Robert A. Proctor— for reading parts of the manuscript and giving valuable criticisms. I am also indebted to Dr. A. V. Washburn, Secretary of the Sunday School Department of the Baptist Sunday School Board, who read most of the manuscript and gave helpful suggestions. Miss Clara McCartt rendered invaluable service in editorial assistance and matters of style. To her I express my profound thanks.

To the students I have taught and who in turn have taught me I express my gratitude. They should be listed as co-authors of this book. I am indebted to Mrs. Glenn Hinson for typing the manuscript. And last, but by no means least, I want to express my appreciation to my wife, Louvenia Littleton Edge, and to my two boys, Larry and Hoyt, for their understanding, interest, and encouragement while this book was being written.

Unit I

Helping the Teacher Plan a Lesson

1. Toward Teacher Improvement

Sincere and devoted teachers meet with Sunday school classes Sunday after Sunday to share their Christian experience and to try to teach the Bible in a meaningful way. They want to be effective teachers, yet they know their teaching falls far short of what it should be. They want to do better—but how? Effective teaching is at the very heart of all the churches are seeking to do. Church buildings are erected, visitation programs are promoted, people are enlisted, literature is published, organization is maintained—all for the purpose that through the preaching and teaching of the Word people might come to know Jesus Christ as Saviour and that they might increasingly grow in his likeness. How to help volunteer lay leadership improve their teaching ministry is a problem which cries for solution.

Areas in which Teachers Need Help

This book seeks to give guidance to the teacher only in the area of techniques of teaching. While the "how" of teaching is a matter of deepest importance and while improvement here is greatly needed, this is not the only area in which the teacher needs help. As the pastor, minister of education, general superintendent, or department superintendent contemplates the total curriculum that should be taught, he will find that there are at least four major areas that ought to be included.

Bible knowledge.—The Bible is the central textbook of the Sunday school. While it is true that a knowledge of the facts of

3

the Bible is not the major objective of Christian teaching, all will agree that the people called by the name Christian ought to have a familiarity with and an understanding of the Bible. Yet there is an appalling lack of Bible knowledge even on the part of many of those who have attended Sunday school regularly. One would expect that after a person has studied the Bible each week for five, ten, or twenty years, he would have a fairly comprehensive grasp of its content and meaning. Yet such is often not the case.

There are probably two reasons for this situation. First, the Bible is not taught with a view to leading the class members to acquire a mastery of its content. In many adult departments the Bible is taught in a devotional manner and the mastery of Bible content almost wholly ignored. In the second place, and equally important, Sunday school members are not led in a serious, systematic study of Bible content because the teachers themselves do not have a sufficient grasp of Bible knowledge to lead such a study.

What is meant by "a serious, systematic study of the Bible" leading to a mastery of its content? A person who has attended Sunday school for a number of years has studied the life of Christ time and time again. The Uniform Lessons have at least one quarter's lessons each year on the life of Christ. Yet, it would be hard to find a person who could give an outline of the life of Christ even in a most general fashion. Only with knowledge of the social, political, economic, and spiritual conditions that Jesus faced can an understanding of the true meaning of the Scriptures come. Or, if consideration is limited to a knowledge of the content of the Bible itself, how many members would have any knowledge of the general outline of the book of Isaiah, or of Jeremiah, or of any of the major or minor prophets? Though knowledge of the content of the Bible is not the major objective of teaching, it is a worthy objective that has not been sufficiently emphasized.

One reason teachers have not led their members in such a

4

study of the Bible is they themselves do not have sufficient understanding and knowledge. This is not a criticism of the teachers. It is simply to call attention to an area where the teachers need help. No one plan alone will be sufficient to give the teachers the mastery of the Bible they want and need. They will have to take advantage of numerous opportunities offered by the church. Books dealing specifically with Bible study are available to teachers. Bible commentaries and other helps make home study more profitable.

In addition to all of these there will be times when the teachers will need to emphasize the study and mastery of Bible content during the teaching improvement period of the weekly officers and teachers' meeting. This may be done quite effectively when the teachers decide to have a "knowledge aim" for a group of lessons. Planned in this way, the Bible content studied on Wednesday night will be directly related to the lesson the teacher will teach on Sunday. It must be emphasized that this Bible study will not be devotional in nature; rather, it will be a serious, systematic—even scholarly—study with a view to understanding meaning and mastering content.

Theology.—The average teacher is often frightened by the word "theology." When he hears the word, he almost invariably thinks of a highly technical, theoretical study dealing with abstract and nebulous ideas. When the suggestion is made that he ought to give more attention to theology in his study and teaching, he almost invariably says, "I leave theology for the scholars and the theologians. I don't deal with theology in my teaching."

However, this statement is not quite accurate. First, every person has a theology. Every person who has done any thinking at all believes something about God; he believes something about Jesus Christ; he believes something about the Bible. This is theology. It may be that his theology is not systematized. It may be that he cannot state it very clearly. But if he believes something about God and life he has a theology. Every Christian ought to be concerned about whether his theology is in harmony with the teaching of the Bible.

The second thing that ought to be said is this: Every Sunday school teacher teaches theology, no matter how much he may protest to the contrary. Every time he talks about God, every time he talks about Jesus, the Bible, faith, or love, he is teaching theology. Therefore the Christian teacher ought to be deeply concerned about whether his statements are based upon a sound interpretation of the biblical revelation.

Sunday school teachers are among the most important teachers of theology in a church. These teachers must recognize their need for help in this area. Church leaders must make plans to give their teachers the help they need. Teachers will find the denominational training course books of tremendous value. They ought to master these books in church and associational training courses, in departmental study groups, and in home study. Other helpful books are W. T. Conner's *The Gospel of Redemption* and John Whale's *Christian Doctrine*.

The pastor has a marvelous opportunity to help his teachers and the church membership at large as he leads his people in doctrinal studies, in training courses, in sermons, and in prayer meetings. There should be no basic conflict between theology taught in the Sunday school and that preached in the pulpit. When this conflict does arise, it is often due to the fact that the Sunday school teacher does not have an intelligent understanding of the teaching of the Bible. This is not the fault of the teacher. Rather it is the fault of those who are responsible for training the teacher.

The weekly officers and teachers' meeting may be used at times to give help to teachers in this area. When a series of lessons are on the great doctrines of the Christian faith, the teachers may be led in a serious study of these doctrines before the lessons are taught. Teachers should be sure their own minds are clear as to the theological implications of the lessons they are to teach.

6

Age-group characteristics.—Teachers also need help in understanding the characteristics of the age group they teach. Perhaps in the past more emphasis has been placed here than has been given to the two areas previously discussed. However, there is continuing need for teachers to understand the pupils they teach. Really effective teaching cannot be done except in terms of the interests, needs, and characteristics of the individuals being taught. The teacher must be keenly aware of the religious concepts the members of his class can grasp at their particular age. Sometimes teachers seek to teach religious concepts which it is impossible for a child to understand at that particular stage of his development.

In understanding the age group he teaches, the teacher will again find the denominational training course books indispensable. He will also be greatly helped if he can attend a state or denominational clinic or assembly. On occasion a study of age-group characteristics may be made at the weekly officers and teachers' meeting. Only rarely will this study need to take up the entire teaching improvement period. However, a brief period (eight to ten minutes) may be used to study one characteristic. Then, as the teachers plan next Sunday's lesson together, they can apply the study they have just made.

Techniques of teaching.—The teacher also needs guidance in teaching techniques. Skillful use of these techniques will help the teacher to make more meaningful and effective the Bible knowledge taught, deepen understanding of the essential meaning of the Scriptures, change attitudes, and enrich lives. It is with this fourth area that this book is concerned.

Various Approaches to Teacher Training

It is relatively easy to point out the areas in which teachers have need. It is also relatively easy to find resource materials to serve as the basis for teacher training. It is far more difficult to provide for teachers those training experiences which will lead them to become increasingly effective channels through whom the message of the Gospel may flow intelligently and meaningfully. Presented here are eleven plans for teacher training. Ten will be presented only briefly. The eleventh will be presented in more detail because it seems to be the best plan for continuous, in-service training. However, it should be understood that no one plan is adequate to meet the needs of any church. All of the plans have their strengths and weaknesses, their advantages and limitations. The best approach to teacher training will use a number of these plans at various times and in various ways.

Apprenticeships.—A promising prospective teacher is asked to work and share experiences with a capable, trained teacher under actual working conditions. Ideally the "apprentice" shares with the teacher in planning the lesson, observes the class experience, and has a conference of analysis and evaluation after each teaching session.

Special training class on Sunday morning.—This class meets during the regular Sunday school hour. A limited number of prospective teachers are invited to enroll in the class. The course of study may last from three months to six months. They are led in a study of Bible content, doctrine, age-group characteristics, and ways of teaching. During the course they are given an opportunity to visit classes of the age group in which they are interested to observe and to have actual teaching experiences.

Training schools.—There are several types of training schools with which most people are familiar. There is the local church training school, the city-wide, the associational, or the regional training school. These may be one-class schools with all teachers meeting together, or they may be multiple-class schools divided either on a department basis or on the basis of different interest groups.

Summer assemblies.—At state and denominational assemblies an opportunity is provided for a concentrated emphasis on leadership development. In these assemblies the leadership is usually the best available, and thus study opportunities are provided under the direction of well trained specialists.

Home study.—Local churches and some denominations are providing guided reading courses for their teachers and other workers. This plan has the advantage of permitting the teacher to study at his own convenience. Its weakness is that it does not provide the personal guidance of a more experienced person which is often so essential to learning.

Monthly workers' conference.—These are regular meetings each month of all the Sunday school teachers and officers. The workers may meet together in one group or they may meet by departments. Too often these meetings are given entirely to matters of organization and promotion. However, some churches have a two-hour session with one hour or more given to training.

Observation.—Opportunities for observation may be provided in the home church, or permission may be secured to observe the work in a class or department of some other church that is doing good work. Best results are secured when the observer knows exactly what to look for.

The helping teacher or supervisor.—In some denominations churches are coming to use what may be called a "helping teacher" or "supervisor." This is a member of the church who by ability and special training is qualified for counseling, observation, and demonstration. Recently the Seabury Press published a *Teacher Training Guide* for the "helping teacher" to use with individuals and groups.

Laboratory schools.—These schools combine classwork with observation of experienced teachers as they work with groups of children in actual teaching situations. They are usually held in the summer and may last from one to three weeks. Sometimes they are held on a series of week ends.

Workshops or retreats.—Many churches have had happy experiences with a week-end retreat for all the officers and teachers before the fall program begins. At this time central problems are considered as they relate to the teaching task of the church. Resources for solving the problems and meeting the challenge are sought and discovered as they relate both to the work of the Sunday school as a whole and to each teacher's task.

A Continuous School

Although these plans are possibilities, the weekly officers and teachers' meeting offers the best opportunity for effective teacher training. It is possible to make the teaching improvement period of the teachers' meeting a "continuous school for teacher improvement." To provide part of the "content" or "curriculum" of this "school" is the purpose of this book. Fortunately, this "school" meets each week. The study may continue week after week, allowing the teachers time to study in a more thorough and leisurely manner. Through the weekly officers and teachers' meeting they can study, learn, and improve as long as they teach.

In the teaching improvement period there is need for variety of approach. All the needs of the teachers cannot be met by any one approach. As the teachers improve their teaching through a study of teaching techniques, they will also improve their knowledge of the Bible and deepen their understanding of theology as they study the Sunday school lesson week by week. Yet there are times when major areas of Bible knowledge and doctrines ought to be given specific and concentrated attention.

Further, any one approach, regardless of how good it may be, if it is used all of the time, will become monotonous. For this reason it is suggested that a study of teaching techniques be planned for a given period of time, perhaps from three to six months. Another period of time may be given to a mastery of Bible knowledge. Following this a study of theology may be made. The type of Sunday school lessons to be taught at a particular time and the personal needs and interests of the teachers should determine what emphasis ought to be followed. Such a program will make the teaching improvement period a continuous school in which Sunday school teachers become better teachers.

The Teaching Improvement Period

The logical question that now arises is what specific plan should be followed to make the weekly officers and teachers' meeting a "continuous school." The most effective way to use the teaching improvement period is for the group study leader to present briefly a study of some technique of teaching. He should then give the teachers an opportunity to "practice" using this technique as they prepare the lesson for the following Sunday. The practice period under the supervision of a study leader will prove most helpful in teaching the teachers to use a given technique.

The group study leader takes the initiative in guiding the teachers to work out a course of study. The remainder of this book provides both guidance and material for such a course of study. The teachers may select from the topics discussed those which meet their most immediate needs. In the main, the topics may be used in any order desired. The material given usually is more than can be covered in the brief period on one Wednesday night. Thus a given topic may be discussed for two or more Wednesday nights. Along with each topic, suggestions are given to the group study leader showing how the teachers may be helped to relate the material to the lesson they are to teach on Sunday.

The group study leader.—The responsibility of leading the teachers in a given department in this study belongs to the department superintendent. The department superintendent is concerned with the organization and administration of his department. He is concerned also with promotion, seeking to reach more people for Bible study. However, his major concern ought to be with the quality of teaching that is done in his department. Therefore, this matter of helping his teachers become better teachers is one of his major responsibilities and opportunities.

It may be that "teaching ability" should be added to the list of qualifications for department superintendents. Usually these

11

officers are chosen for their organizational, administrative, and promotional abilities. To improve the quality of teaching in Sunday schools, superintendents who have the highest teaching ability need to be selected. The superintendent should be the best teacher in the department. Unfortunately this opportunity of the superintendent has not been sufficiently emphasized in the past. One often hears the remark from a teacher who has become a department superintendent, "I enjoy my work as superintendent, but I surely do miss my work as a teacher." What he fails to recognize is that as superintendent he has a greater opportunity to teach than he had as the teacher of a class. As superintendent he has the opportunity to help lift the level of the quality of all the teaching that is done in his department by becoming the "teacher of his teachers." He has no greater opportunity nor heavier responsibility than this. Therefore it is his task to lead his teachers in the study of teaching techniques and to lead them in applying these principles as they prepare the lesson they are to teach on Sunday.

In those departments where the superintendent does not have teaching ability, it perhaps will be necessary for the superintendent and teachers to select by common agreement one of the teachers in the department who has unusual teaching ability. However, if at all possible, the department superintendent ought to assume this responsibility.

The plan.—On Wednesday night the department superintendent presents to his teachers the teaching technique that is to be considered for that night. This presentation will be as brief as possible to allow time for practice in using the technique as the teachers prepare the lesson for Sunday. The problem of time is one of the most difficult. If the teaching improvement period is only thirty minutes, as is often the case, the study-leader will have only seven or eight minutes to present the technique. The remaining twenty-two or twenty-three minutes will have to be reserved for the application of the technique in lesson preparation. A teaching improvement period of from forty-five minutes to one hour is desperately needed. The follow-ing schedule is suggested for consideration:

6:00 Meal
6:30 General promotional period
6:45 Department promotional period
7:00 Department teaching improvement period
8:00 Prayer meeting

If this schedule is followed, the department superintendent would have twenty to twenty-five minutes to present the educa-tional technique, and the teachers would have from thirty-five to forty minutes for application and lesson preparation.

A word of explanation is needed about "application of the teaching technique in lesson preparation." After the superin-tendent has presented the teaching technique (or some part of it), he should then guide the teachers in their lesson prepara-tion for Sunday, leading them to apply the technique that was studied. For example, the group is studying the topic "Using the Question and Answer Method." The superintendent would present this topic, helping the teachers to understand it fully and answering questions they might have about it. He would then lead the teachers to begin the preparation of the lesson for Sunday. During this preparation of the lesson he would en-courage the teachers to plan the questions they might ask on Sunday. He would help them analyze the type of questions to be asked and evaluate their possible effectiveness.

The department superintendent may find it necessary to spend two or more Wednesday nights on a topic such as ques-tions and answers. Actually this is not a disadvantage but rather an advantage. In the first place, with the limited time available, he will find that it will take several weeks in order to give a satisfactory presentation of the educational principle being studied. In the second place, the teachers should have a num-ber of weeks in which to practice using the technique so that it will become so much a part of their experience they will be able to apply it in any subsequent lesson they might teach. The idea behind this plan is not to see how many principles can be covered in a given amount of time but to stay with a principle until the teachers know how to use it.

It will be noted that when the teachers begin their lesson preparation a study group procedure is used, with each teacher actively participating. The department superintendent does not teach the lesson for next Sunday. Rather, the teachers sit around a table where they can write and talk together. Each teacher should be provided with a mimeographed lesson plan sheet which he can fill out during the discussion. In this discussion each teacher shares his ideas, insights, and experiences. Obviously it is necessary for each teacher to study the lesson before he comes on Wednesday night in order to have something to share.

The size of this study group is important. It is necessary that the group be small enough for each teacher to get individual attention from the leader. Unfortunately, there are some superintendents and teachers who feel that they cannot have a good meeting unless there is a large group. But when we are teaching skills, it is important that each one get individual attention. From five to seven persons make the best number for a study group. If there are as many as fifteen to eighteen teachers in a department, it would be wise to make two or three study groups. Otherwise, some of the teachers will be lost in the group; usually these will be the ones who most need help.

Advantages

This plan of using the study of a teaching technique with practice in applying it in lesson preparation has several advantages. First, it gives the teachers an opportunity to improve the quality of their teaching by making an intensive study of ways of teaching. Sunday school teachers are housewives, secretaries, lawyers, farmers, businessmen, and laborers. Most of them have never made a serious study of the matter of teaching. They

14

want to be effective teachers, but they need help. This plan seeks to provide the help needed. Second, it provides guidance for the teacher in the preparation of the lesson he is to teach on Sunday. When the entire teachers' meeting is used for a study of educational principles, teachers complain that they do not get the specific help needed for teaching next Sunday's lesson. This new plan combines a study of the teaching technique with a study of the lesson to be taught on Sunday.

Third, it not only provides the teachers with an opportunity to study principles of teaching but it also gives them an opportunity to practice using the principles in working out an actual lesson. Too often efforts to train teachers have been too theoretical and abstract. Leaders have sought to teach methods of teaching, but the studies have not been related to an actual teaching experience. As a result, when the teacher found these principles difficult to apply in lesson preparation, he tended to continue teaching as though he never had the course of study. The plan suggested herein avoids that pitfall by providing the teacher an opportunity to apply the principle as he plans his lesson under the supervision and guidance of the study leader.

Fourth, this plan also has the advantage of utilizing the technique of "on the job training." The teachers' study of an educational technique is not knowledge stored up for future use. They put it into practice immediately in preparing the lesson; they try it out in an actual situation on Sunday; and on the following Wednesday night, they analyze and discuss the successes and failures of Sunday. Then they make plans to do a better job of teaching next Sunday.

Fifth, when the weekly officers and teachers' meeting is used as a school for teacher improvement, the teachers have a school that continues indefinitely. This is a distinct advantage. In a regular Sunday school training course study that meets for five nights during the week the teacher of the course feels that he has to cover a certain amount of material. He does not have time to lead the teachers in a leisurely practice and application of the principles being studied. Even when a study is given during the weekly teachers' meeting, the leader feels he has to cover a given number of topics in a given amount of time. However, in this plan no one should be in a rush to cover a given number of topics in a given amount of time. If, in a three-months period, the group has studied only four topics, that is quite satisfactory provided those four topics have been mastered by the teachers. If the teachers for the sake of variety want to have some other type of study that too is quite satisfactory. The weekly officers and teachers' meeting continues indefinitely. Eventually the department superintendent will have time to teach all the teaching techniques presented in this book and many more! Don't rush. Make mastery the purpose.

Sixth, this plan has in it those principles which are conducive to learning: (1) The teachers have a sense of need—they have to teach the lesson for next Sunday. (2) They have an interest —they want to improve. (3) They have an opportunity to learn through doing. (4) They have an opportunity to put into practice what they have studied by using it in teaching on Sunday. (5) They have an opportunity for review and evaluation when they come together the following Wednesday night.

2. Steps in Preparing a Lesson

A CAREFULLY PREPARED LESSON PLAN is indispensable for effective teaching. What a map is to a traveler, what a blueprint is to a builder, what a sketch is to an artist, a lesson plan is to a teacher. In this course of study the steps in a lesson plan are considered first because it is essential that the teacher have a systematic approach to lesson preparation if he is to improve his teaching. The various techniques of teaching that are considered later in this book will fit normally and naturally into the lesson plan to be suggested here.

The Importance of Planning

Why this concern about lesson plans and lesson preparation? Why is it necessary for the teacher to spend so much time, energy, and effort in planning? Is not teaching a rather simple thing? Is there not enough material in the quarterly? Why can't the teacher merely "give" it to the class? Teaching is not "dishing" out material as a cook dishes out food. Teaching is using the living Word to confront people with the redeeming God in such a way that the Holy Spirit has an effective opportunity to make the Word come alive in the life of the learner. This is neither easy nor simple. There is no more important task in which the teacher may engage. It demands the best, both in preparation and life, that any teacher has to offer. Surely he cannot offer to God nor to his members a haphazard, slipshod, half-prepared lesson.

The teacher's time for teaching is, at best, limited. The lesson must be planned to make the most effective use of the time available. The teacher must not be satisfied with simply reading the lesson, getting a general familiarity with the ideas presesented, making a few hastily prepared notes on a piece of paper, or worse yet, on the margin of his quarterly, and using these as the basis for teaching. The task of the teacher is far too sacred and the lives of his class members far too important for him to make such an unworthy approach. It takes time to plan, but the teacher must be willing to give sufficient time and effort for adequate preparation.

A lesson plan serves many purposes for the teacher. It helps him determine what material should be used and what material has to be left out. It gives him a sense of confidence as he comes before his class on Sunday morning. It helps the teacher and the class to "keep on the track" and avoid meaningless discussion. It helps guide the teacher in determining the amount of time to be given to each part of the lesson. However, the teacher must not be a slave to his lesson plan. The plan must be flexible enough to allow the teacher to leave it temporarily to follow pupil interest. The teacher must remember that achieving the objective is the important matter in teaching. If the class members need to go down another path, or if they need to spend more time on a problem than the teacher had planned, and if this change will better achieve the objective, the lesson plan should be modified and sometimes completely discarded.

Practical Aids

There are certain simple, practical matters that will aid the teacher in his lesson preparation.

Time for preparation.—Everyone is busy. Yet it is true that busy people usually find time to do more things than those who are not so busy. Perhaps the reason is that busy people have learned how to schedule their activities. The busy teacher must put a definite time (or times) in his weekly schedule for lesson preparation. These times for study should be guarded as carefully and kept as faithfully as an engagement with an important friend. If the weekly officers and teachers' meeting is to be used as a school in which the teachers plan next Sunday's lesson together, it is absolutely necessary for the teacher to study the lesson *before* the meeting on Wednesday. This is necessary for two reasons: First, the study of the lesson at the teachers' meeting will not be as helpful if the lesson has not been studied ahead of time. Second, if he has not studied the lesson, he will have nothing to contribute to the group discussion.

The teacher will want to make a preliminary study of the quarter's lessons before the quarter begins. Such a study gives him a general familiarity with the lessons to be taught. He will begin specific preparation for a particular lesson on Sunday or Monday. Further study will be done on Wednesday night at the teachers' meeting, and his concluding preparation will be made later in the week.

Place for preparation.—Many teachers find it helpful to have a definite place for lesson preparation. The Bible, lesson quarterlies, other lesson helps, pupil notebooks, commentaries, and other aids are kept in this place so that they are available when needed.

Materials for preparation.—What materials does the teacher need to help him in his lesson preparation? He will, of course, start with his Bible. Perhaps he will want two Bibles to aid him in his study—one a good modern translation. Then he will need the teacher's quarterly and the pupil's quarterly. He needs to know what the class members have studied. There are other lesson helps which are prepared annually on the basis of the Uniform Lesson Series. *Broadman Comments* and *Rozell's Complete Lessons* are two of the best. He will need his notebook with information concerning his class members, because every lesson must be prepared with the needs and interests of the members in mind.

The teacher will need at least a good one-volume commentary. Dummelow's *A Commentary on the Whole Bible* and

Jamieson, Fausset, and Brown's *A Commentary Critical and Explanatory on the Whole Bible* are good. The teacher also needs a Bible dictionary. *The Westminister Dictionary of the Bible* and *Hastings' Dictionary of the Bible* are good. Another important aid in lesson preparation is a Bible atlas. *The Westminister Historical Atlas to the Bible* is good.

Background Preparation

Personal preparation.—As the teacher approaches the study of the lesson his own spiritual attitude is quite important. Therefore his preparation must begin with himself through prayer and meditation. The teacher does not study or teach alone. The Holy Spirit is the teacher's guide and teacher. Yet it is necessary for the teacher to have "ears that hear" when the Holy Spirit speaks. If the teacher is tired, or distraught, or if the cares of the day press upon him, it may be difficult for God's message to get through. Lesson study is a holy time and should be approached in a spirit of deepest reverence.

Studying the Bible.—In attempting to prepare the lesson, what should the teacher do first? What should he do next? The steps will vary with different teachers. Each one should follow the approach that is most helpful to him. The following is merely suggestive. It should be noted that these steps are not separate, air-tight compartments; they overlap and interlace with one another in one continuous process. They are separated here only for the purpose of letting the teacher take a look at them. First, he may read from the Bible the Scripture passage that is printed in the quarterly and the context (larger lesson) in which the printed passage is found. In this first reading of the Scripture passage the teacher should let the Bible speak to him. He reads for his own spiritual enrichment. What is God saying to him in this passage? What have the truths in this passage meant to his own personal life? What are some of the problems he still faces?

Next, the teacher will want to study the passage a second time, using a commentary to help him understand the meaning of the Scripture passage. In this study the teacher is not looking for "applications" of the lesson. He is seeking the essential meaning of the passage. Along with this he will want to look up unfamiliar words or places in a Bible dictionary or atlas.

Having done this, the teacher will read the lesson exposition in the teacher's quarterly to see the emphasis that has been given to the passage in this lesson. Other lesson helps will also be used at this point.

Considering the class members.—After he has sought to master the essential meaning of the Scripture passage, the teacher will want to take a look at the members of his class. It is necessary for the teacher to adapt each lesson to his particular class. This means that it is absolutely essential for him to know the members of his class. He will need to know more about them than just their names, addresses, and birthdays. It also means that small classes are necessary because teachers do not teach classes. They teach individuals. What needs do these members have that are met by this lesson? On the basis of the teacher's study of the Bible passage and on the basis of his consideration of the needs of his members, the teacher is now ready to determine his aim for the lesson.

A Lesson Plan Outline [1]

Teachers often ask, "Is there a plan or an outline that will give me guidance as I prepare the lesson?" Actually there are almost as many different ways of planning a lesson as there are teachers. Lesson plans vary as to emphasis. One plan emphasizes content and organization of material. Another plan may emphasize the needs of the members. Still another may emphasize materials and methods to be used. Lesson plans vary as to age groups. Small children are taught through centers of activity. Older children may have an "early time" or a "pre-class session."

---

[1] For a more comprehensive discussion of each of these steps in the suggested plan see Findley B. Edge, *Teaching for Results* (Nashville: Broadman Press, 1956), pp. 89–166.

Lesson plans also vary as to purpose. If the teacher has a conduct response aim, he might use one plan. For a knowledge aim, he probably would use a different plan.[2] However, it cannot be emphasized too strongly that it is essential for the teacher to follow some plan in lesson preparation, either the one suggested here or one of his own choosing. The five divisions of the lesson plan are:

Selecting an aim.—The teacher should plan his aims in terms of knowledge, inspiration, or conduct response, depending on the results he is seeking. The aim should be clearly stated and sufficiently specific for him to have a possibility of achieving his objective. This will include quarterly, unit, and lesson aims.

Securing purposeful Bible study.—The teacher should plan how he will secure class interest at the beginning of the lesson in order to lead the group in a meaningful and serious study of the Bible.

Developing the lesson.—In developing the lesson the teacher will try to lead the class to understand the meaning of the Scripture and to understand and accept the general Christian ideal taught. He will need to consider what will be the most effective arrangement of the material to be taught, the methods to be used, and what materials (such as pictures or maps) will be needed.

Making the lesson personal.—The teacher must lead each member to see and to face frankly how the spiritual ideal being considered relates to his own personal life. To do this in a meaningful manner is the problem of this part of the lesson plan.

Securing carry-over.—How can the teacher keep the lesson from ending in just "talk"? He should lead the class to consider not only what they *ought* to do but also what they *will* do.

The teachers should have a lesson plan sheet to guide them in their lesson preparation. It would look something like this:

---

[2] The lesson plan suggested here is to be used with lessons having a conduct response aim. The lesson plan to be used with lessons having a knowledge aim is suggested in chapter four.

Lesson Plan For Conduct Response Aim

1. Aim for quarter:
   (4 spaces)
2. Aim for unit:
   (4 spaces)
3. Aim for lesson:
   (4 spaces)
4. Securing purposeful Bible study:
   (1) To secure interest:
       (4 spaces)
   (2) Transition:
       (3 spaces)
   (3) What to look for as Bible is read:
       (4 spaces)
5. Developing the lesson:
   (14 spaces)
6. Making the lesson personal:
   (10 spaces)
7. Securing carry-over:
   (the remainder of the page)

This or a similar lesson plan should be mimeographed on paper 8½ inches x 11 inches for the teachers to use on Wednesday night in their lesson preparation. As they study the lesson together, they will write in the points, illustrations, and questions they plan to use in teaching the lesson. At the close of the study period each teacher should have at least a rough draft of the lesson he is to teach on Sunday.

Selecting Aims

We come now (in the remainder of this chapter and in the next chapter) to a brief consideration of each of the steps in this lesson plan.[3] One of the most serious weaknesses of modern Sun-

---

[3] The teachers could well spend one or more Wednesday nights in studying and coming to master each of these steps. That is, one or more nights may be spent studying "Selecting Aims"; one or more nights may be spent studying "How to Secure Purposeful Bible Study." Actually, the study of the material given in this chapter and the next chapter might cover ten or more weeks.

day school teaching is in the area of aims. Too often little is learned or little happens as the result of the study of a Sunday school lesson because the teacher was not sure what he wanted the class to learn or what he wanted to happen. In other words, the teacher did not have the lesson aim clearly in mind. Choosing the aim is one of the most difficult parts of the whole lesson plan. Many teachers fail to recognize this. Too often they have not given sufficient consideration to the selection of their aims; neither have they understood how aims ought to be selected and stated. As a result their teaching has lacked the effectiveness it might have had.

In selecting an aim the teacher must begin with the Scripture passage. The lesson aim should grow out of the meaning of the Bible passage. The aim must also be related to the needs of the members of the class. Only the teacher knows the specific needs of his particular class. For this reason lesson writers can rarely determine what the teacher's aim ought to be. They can state the aim only in the most general terms since they are writing for thousands of classes. Therefore it is almost always necessary for the teacher to adapt any suggested aim and make it more specific in terms of the needs of his particular class.

What are the qualities of a good aim? There are at least three. First, an aim should be brief enough to be remembered. The aim is what the teacher wants the members to learn or to do as the result of the lesson study. If the aim is so long that the teacher cannot remember it, how can he expect the members of the class to remember it? Second, the aim ought to be clear enough to be written down. Too often teachers have only a vague, hazy idea of the lesson aim. If they were asked to express this aim in words, they would find it difficult if not impossible to do so. Third, the aim ought to be specific enough to be attainable. As a rule the aims teachers select are far too broad and general. The teacher must remember that he probably will have only thirty minutes in which to teach the lesson. He ought to be more humble in what he seeks to achieve in a given lesson and select an aim that is sufficiently specific. It should be small enough to at least have the possibility of being achieved within the time limits of the particular lesson. More will be said about this when we consider lesson aims.

Quarterly Aims

The teacher needs to see the quarter's lessons as a whole. For thirteen weeks he will have the opportunity of guiding the thinking of his class. What does he want to accomplish in these thirteen weeks? If his aim is not clear, his teaching will usually be equally vague. How can the teacher accomplish his objective if he does not know clearly and specifically what his objective is?

Many times a teacher comes to the end of a quarter with little or no sense of achievement. No wonder teaching becomes a bore and a drag for him. He has no real thrill of achievement! At the end of a quarter he asks himself, "What, specifically, have I accomplished in the lives of my class members through this quarter's lesson?" And he has to content himself with the vague hope that he has done some good.

Why is this true? It may be that the teacher taught each lesson as an end in itself, wholly unrelated to the lesson that was taught last Sunday and to that which will be taught the following Sunday. On the other hand, if, before the quarter began, the teacher had written down a clear, definite aim for the quarter and then for thirteen weeks taught, Sunday after Sunday, with each lesson planned to achieve that objective, he would have a far better chance of achieving his over-all objective. In this approach each lesson is built on the preceding lesson and points to the aim the teacher has selected for the quarter. The quarterly aim should of course be worked out before the quarter begins, perhaps as the teachers are led in a preview study of the quarter's lessons.

Some teachers relate each lesson to the preceding lesson by reviewing briefly the lesson for last Sunday. This plan is not the only way, nor necessarily the best way, to relate preceding lessons to the present lesson. Sometimes this review may not come until the class is in the middle of the current lesson. As some problem is raised, the teacher may lead the class to recall last Sunday's lesson or some other lesson to help solve the current problem. This makes the review of the preceding lessons a vital and meaningful part of the present lesson, not merely a mechanical device used to get started.

Following is an example of a quarterly aim for an adult class: "My aim for this quarter is to lead my members to find one new way to express their Christian faith (1) in their home life, (2) in their business life, and (3) in their social life." Here the teacher has three specific objectives (they will be made even more specific when we consider unit aims) he wants to accomplish. Thus he will be able to make each lesson contribute to the achieving of one of these purposes. If the teacher has such a plan in mind at the beginning of the quarter, he has a much better chance of realizing success at the end of the quarter.

Unit Aims

A unit aim is one which the teacher has for a group of two or more lessons that go together naturally. As the teacher studies the lessons for the quarter, he will find that a certain group of lessons can be used to accomplish the same objective. This becomes the unit aim. Using the quarter's aim given above, "To lead my members to find one new way to express their Christian faith (1) in their home life, (2) in their business life, and (3) in their social life," the teacher would have three unit aims. The aim for unit one, related to home life, might be "To lead my members to start a family altar." The aim for unit two, related to business life, might be "To lead my members to witness for Christ in their business contacts, using a plan similar to 'desk top witnessing.'" The aim for unit three, related to social life, might be, "To lead my members to give help to some underprivileged in our community," or "To lead my members to begin positive action against some community social ill."

26

The teacher plans and teaches each lesson to accomplish this unit objective. With specific aims such as these in mind the teacher, at the end of each unit and at the end of each quarter, can look at the lives of his members and with more accuracy tell to what extent he has been successful in achieving his aim. Thus specific quarterly and unit aims give the teacher a basis for evaluating the effectiveness of his teaching.

A second value of teaching with unit aims clearly in mind is that it gives the teacher an opportunity to use repetition in his teaching. Repetition is a basic principle in teaching and in learning. The mother does not expect the child to say thank you simply because she has told him one time to say it. Most of the major matters of life are learned through repeated impact. Teachers must realize that a major spiritual truth is rarely learned in just one lesson. But by forming a series of lessons into a unit dealing with one spiritual truth, the teacher has an opportunity to confront the class with repeated teaching concerning the truth—its meaning, its message, and its expression. Each lesson will have a different emphasis and a different approach, but the spiritual truth studied will be the same. The teacher will have a much greater possibility of getting results, both in learning and in life, if unit planning is followed.

Lesson Aims

As a general rule the teacher has three objectives in mind when he teaches. He seeks (1) to teach knowledge, (2) to inspire his class, and (3) to secure a conduct response. Some teachers undertake to accomplish all three of these objectives in the same lesson. This is one of the major reasons Sunday school teaching is not any more effective than it is. If the teacher is to secure more results either in the amount of Bible knowledge learned, or in terms of attitudes deepened, or in terms of Christian living, he must select one of these aims, and only one, *for a given lesson* and seek only that one with all his heart.

If a teacher desires to have his class to learn more Bible knowledge (and in the light of the woeful ignorance of the Bible this is greatly needed) there are lessons for which he should have a knowledge aim and seek only to lead the class to understand and master this knowledge. If he desires to deepen the commitment of his members in terms of a given Christian attitude, he should have an inspiration aim and seek that alone. If he wants to lead his members to express in their lives some Christian action, he should have a conduct response aim and seek that alone. When the teacher tries to achieve all three of these objectives in the same lesson, he usually does not achieve adequate results in any one of the three.

Many people have been attending Sunday school for five, ten, and more years yet they have little real, systematic knowledge of the Bible. People who have been coming to Sunday school for years still fail to express in life the great Christian ideals they have studied. This does not mean that they have not enjoyed the lessons. This does not even mean that they have not agreed with the lessons. It simply means they have not adequately expressed the Christian gospel in their lives.

Perhaps it would help us see more clearly the difference in these three types of aims if we defined and gave an example of each. A lesson with a knowledge aim [4] is one in which the teacher seeks to lead the class in a serious and systematic study of a significant portion of Bible material leading to a mastery of that knowledge. An example would be "To lead my class to master the events leading up the the Fall of Jerusalem" or "To lead my class to master the essential message of the book of Amos."

A lesson with an inspiration aim is one in which the teacher seeks to lead the class to deepen their appreciation of some Christian truth or to lead them to accept or re-accept some Christian ideal or attitude. An example would be "To lead my class to a deeper appreciation of the Bible as the Word of God"

---

[4] The knowledge aim will be discussed more fully in chapter 4.

or "To lead my class to a deeper faith through a study of the resurrection of Jesus." A lesson with a conduct response aim is one in which the teacher seeks to lead the class to express in a specific way some Christian action in his daily life. An example would be "To lead my class to respond as 'peacemakers' when someone does them an injustice" or "To lead my class to participate in the weekly visitation program of the church."

It is true that these aims are not mutually exclusive, but each is distinctive. For example, if the teacher has a knowledge aim for a given lesson, his members might be inspired through the study, but his aim is not inspiration; his aim is to lead the members to master the material studied. If he has an inspiration aim, the class may gain some knowledge, and they may have some conduct response. If so, this is extra. His aim is to deepen some general attitude. If he has a conduct response aim, it is true that he will have to use some knowledge, for response must always be built upon knowledge; however, two things need to be kept in mind here. First, the knowledge used will not be a systematic study of a significant portion of Scripture. Rather, the knowledge selected will be that which will lead to the response desired. This knowledge may come from various parts of the Bible. In the second place, with a conduct response aim the teacher does not seek to lead the class to a mastery of the knowledge. The aim is the desired response. The knowledge is a means and not the end. With a conduct response aim the class may also be inspired, but the aim has not been achieved until there is an observable response in the lives of the members.

It is highly important that teachers learn to identify these three types of aims. All three types of aims are worthy, and the teacher should use each type of aim—but not in the same lesson. The point is that when a teacher decides what type of lesson he desires for a given Sunday (knowledge, inspiration, conduct response), he should make sure that his statement of aim coincides with the type of lesson he desires. That is, he ought not to confuse a conduct response lesson by having an inspiration aim. The following questions are given to help the teacher identify the different types of aims:

1. Is my primary purpose to teach facts? Is my primary purpose to give information? Is my primary purpose to lead to a mastery of the meaning of the Bible passage? Then I will select a knowledge aim.

2. Is my primary purpose to deepen appreciation in some area? Is my primary purpose to teach some general attitude? Then I will need an inspiration aim.

3. Is my primary purpose to secure some definite response in the life of the members? What is the response? How can it be expressed? Then I will choose a conduct response aim.

As has been stated previously, one of the major weaknesses in Sunday school teaching is that the teacher's aims have been too general. It has also been pointed out that one quality of a good aim is that it be specific enough to be attainable. The question now is how specific a specific aim ought to be. A knowledge aim is made specific by the knowledge the teacher wants the class to master. An inspiration aim can be more general because it deals with a general ideal or attitude. But how specific ought a conduct response aim to be? A conduct response aim ought to be stated in terms of an overt, observable response. There are two questions a teacher ought always to ask when he has a conduct response aim in mind: (1) What do I want my members to do? (2) How can they give expression to the response I want them to make?

In a conduct response lesson the teacher needs to pick out one area in the lives of his members where they are failing to express some Christian ideal which they accept. He then lifts this specific area to the level of consciousness in the class session so the members can look at it. What the Bible has to say is brought to bear upon the problem; the members share their insights, their difficulties, and their experiences. The teacher sheds what light he has upon the problem. Out of this discussion the Holy Spirit has an opportunity to convict of sin. If the conviction is sufficiently deep, changes may take place in the lives of the members as they make a response in life.

It is true that the needs of the members may differ. This means that the teacher may have a different aim for each member, but this also must be specific. Each member may accept a "learning goal" which he chooses for himself and toward which he strives in expressing a Christian ideal.

Let it be stated again that selecting an aim is one of the most difficult and most important parts of the lesson for the teacher to plan. If his thinking is vague and hazy here, his teaching likewise will be vague and hazy and his results limited.

Guidance In Lesson Preparation

At this point the department superintendent is to lead his teachers in the study and preparation of next Sunday's lesson. The following questions will help guide the superintendent:

1. Do the teachers have a definite time (or times) for lesson preparation? Do they need to come to a decision about this matter?

2. When do they begin preparing the lesson for next Sunday? It is absolutely necessary for them to begin preparation before they come on Wednesday night.

3. Do they have a special place where they prepare the lesson? Would this be helpful?

4. What materials do they have to help them in their lesson preparation? Do they need other helps? A commentary? A Bible dictionary? A Bible atlas? Other helps?

5. How do the teachers go about preparing the lesson? What do they do first? What next?

6. What lesson plan do they use? Is the lesson plan suggested in this chapter usable? Does it need to be modified? Should it be mimeographed for the teachers to use each Wednesday night?

Other specific matters ought to be applied as the teachers prepare the lesson. "Quarterly Aims" and "Unit Aims" should be studied near the end of one quarter so the teachers will be able to work out quarterly and unit aims for the next quarter's lessons. This particular study may have to be done at some time other than on Wednesday night—perhaps as the teachers engage in the preview study of the next quarter's lessons.

7. What is the aim for next quarter's lessons? Each teacher should work out his own aim and write it down.

(1) Is it brief enough to be remembered?

(2) Is it clear enough to be written down?

(3) Is it specific enough to be attainable?

8. What are the unit aims for next quarter's lessons? Again each teacher should evaluate the unit aims he has written down.

(1) Is it brief enough to be remembered?

(2) Is it clear enough to be written down?

(3) Is it specific enough to be attainable?

9. What is the aim the teacher plans to use for next Sunday's lesson? Each teacher should write his down.

(1) Is it a knowledge aim? Is the teacher's primary purpose to lead his class to master information?

(2) Is it an inspiration aim? Is the teacher's primary purpose to strengthen some Christian attitude or ideal?

(3) Is it a conduct response aim? Is the teacher's primary purpose to lead his class to make some specific response in life?

(4) Is it brief enough to be remembered?

(5) Is it clear enough to be written down?

(6) Is it specific enough to be attainable?

If the teacher has a conduct response aim in mind there are two more questions that will have to be considered:

(7) What does he want his classes to do?

(8) How can they express their decision?

After each teacher has selected and evaluated his aim, the group should be led in the preparation of the remainder of the lesson they are to teach next Sunday.

3. Teaching for Conduct Response

IN THE PRECEDING CHAPTER we discussed the first step in preparing a lesson—selecting the aim. We come now to consider the remaining four steps in a lesson plan to be used when the teacher's aim is conduct response.

Securing Purposeful Bible Study

After the teacher has selected his aim, he is ready to plan how he will secure a purposeful study of the Bible. This part of the lesson plan usually is referred to as the introduction. This section is not concerned with ways the Bible may be and ought to be used in the development of the lesson. The problem is how the teacher, through a well planned introduction, can lead the class in a meaningful study of the Scripture passage the first time the Scripture passage is read in the class. Of course there will be times when the Bible may not be used until the middle of the lesson. There will be other times when the teacher will want to use only a part of the Scripture passage at the beginning of the lesson and other parts later in the lesson. But whenever and however the Scripture lesson is used, it ought to be used with purpose and have meaning for the members of the class.

Too often this is not the case. Many teachers have developed a routine which they follow Sunday after Sunday. The class comes into the room; they take the records, have a brief prayer, and somebody reads the Scripture lesson. All this is done *before* the teacher begins teaching. And the reading of the Scripture passage, whether it is done by the teacher or by one or more of the members, often has little meaning to the members. This is a poor way for the Bible to be used. Both the fault and the responsibility for changing it lies in the hands of the teacher. Here is a rule which the teacher ought to observe: *Do not read the Bible as the first thing in the class period.* The Bible should be read only after the class has been made ready to read it. What does this mean for the teacher and how is he to help the class to be ready to read the Bible?

Prepare the class.—Before the Bible is read, it is the task of the teacher to stimulate the class to *want* to read it and to give some *purpose* for reading it. This is in opposition to the listless and purposeless way the Bible is read in some classes. This means that the introduction must be planned carefully by the teacher. By well chosen questions, statements, illustrations, or discussion the teacher should seek to stimulate the interest of the class in the problem to be considered. The teacher should seek so to arouse the curiosity and interest of the class that they will develop the attitude, "Let's open the Bible and see what it says." How can this be done?

If the teacher is to get the attention of the class and deepen this attention into interest, he must begin with something that is in line with the normal interests of his class. This is not too difficult because the people of all ages are interested in many things. However, it does take some careful planning on the part of the teacher. The first thing the teacher says in the class will be one of the most important things he will say during the whole period. There is little reason for the teacher to go on teaching the rest of the lesson unless he first captures the interest of the class and leads them to want to take the spiritual journey that has been planned for the class session. As the teacher prepares his lesson, he ought to plan definitely and specifically the very first thing he will say to his class.

If the teacher of Intermediate boys began a lesson by saying, "Today we are going to study about a prophet by the name of Micaiah," the Intermediates probably would not feel a deep sense of excitement and holy expectancy. Would he not have a much better chance of securing their attention if he started by asking, "Why do people tell lies?" Some of the pupils would undoubtedly say to get out of trouble or to escape punishment. The teacher could follow this discussion with another question. "Is it ever right for a person to tell a lie to escape punishment?" After brief comments by the class, the teacher may say, "The person we study about today was faced with that problem. Let's open our Bibles and see what he did."

As the teacher seeks to stimulate the class to want to read the Bible, it is usually better for him to lead the class to make a vocal response. There will be times when the teacher may use an illustration or some other means of securing the interest of the class when the members do not make a response. But as a rule the more the class is brought into active participation by way of vocal response, the deeper will be their interest in what is being discussed.

The introduction the teacher uses to stimulate the interest of the class in the reading of the Scripture must not only be in line with the interest of the class but must also point toward the development of the lesson. The purpose of the introduction is to lead the class to engage in purposeful reading and meaningful discussion of the Bible. It is possible for the teacher to get the attention of the class in a number of ways. He may talk about the party the group had Friday night, or he may talk about politics, or the world situation. These may get the attention and interest of the class, but they may not be in line with the aim or purpose of the lesson.

In the introduction there must also be a transition that leads naturally from that which the teacher uses to secure the interest of the class to the reading of the Bible. The importance of this point cannot be emphasized too strongly. Without a good transition, the class may continue in idle talk. If the teacher plans to secure the interest of the class by talking about the basketball game that was played Friday night, unless he has also planned a transition that will lead naturally from this discussion to a reading of the Bible, the class will keep on talking about the ball game. In the first example given above, the statement, "The person we study about this morning was faced with this problem," is the transition.

Thus there are three points the teacher needs to observe as he seeks to "prepare the class" for the reading of the Scripture. His introduction must (1) be in line with the interest of the class; (2) it must point toward the development of the lesson; and (3) it must have a transition that leads naturally to the reading of the Scripture.

What to look for.—However, the class is still not "ready" to read the Bible. After the teacher has stimulated the interest of the class and *before* the Bible is read, he ought to give the class something specific to look for as the passage is being read. This will focus attention on those things the teacher feels are important for the lesson. If the first part of the introduction is to give purpose for Bible study, this second part is to give direction to Bible study. As the Bible is being read, if no purpose is given and if the reading is not directed, the minds of the class members will tend to wander. However, if the teacher directs the minds of the members by telling them some specific things to look for, the reading of the Scripture will be much more meaningful. The class will be searching for answers and not merely listening.

In directing the reading of the Bible passage the teacher should use variety. Certainly he should not do it the same way every Sunday. Sometimes he may use questions. At other times he may ask the members to pick out the key verse in the passage, or to note the emphasis given a certain matter in the Scripture. The teacher will plan variety in line with what he wants the class to note. The important thing is to make sure the class understands clearly what they are to look for as the Bible is being read. The questions must also be in line with the age group being taught. On the one hand they should not be so simple as to insult the intelligence of the class, and on the other, they should not be so difficult the class cannot find the answer.

Read the Scripture passage.—After the class has been prepared for the reading of the Scripture, after the members have been led to want to read it, after they have been given a purpose for reading it, after they have been told what to look for, then the Bible should be read—not before. The question is often asked: Should the teacher read the passage, or should he ask a member to read it? Again, variety should be used. There are times when the teacher should read; at other times, a member might read. The important thing is that, whoever reads it, the Bible should be read with understanding and meaning. Many passages of Scripture are difficult to read. Far too often the Bible is read poorly and haltingly with seemingly no understanding of its meaning. If a member is going to read, he should be told in advance in order that he may be prepared to read well. With younger groups the teacher should even go over the Scripture with the class member. It is necessary that the passage be read with proper emphasis and with an understanding of its meaning.

Answers to questions.—Do not ask the class members to note something or to look for something and then not ask them about it. If the questions have been carefully selected, the discussion of the answers should lead naturally into the development of the lesson.

A few general suggestions will be helpful to the teacher as he seeks to introduce the lesson so as to secure a purposeful study of the Bible. First, he must have variety in his approach. Second, he should seek to make his introduction as stimulating as possible. Third, in the introduction it is not the task of the teacher to tell the class what is in the passage; rather, it is his task to lead them to want to see what the passage says. Fourth, he should avoid having a long, involved, and complex introduction. Finally, in his lesson preparation the teacher should plan his introduction almost word for word. That is, he should plan exactly the first thing he is going to say when he begins his teaching on Sunday. He should forecast the probable response his members will make.

Developing the Lesson

The development of the lesson is that portion sometimes referred to as the body of the lesson. In terms of time it consumes the major portion of the teaching period. This indicates something of its importance.

Purpose of the development.—What is it the teacher seeks to do in the development of the lesson? First, he seeks to lead the class to understand the meaning of the Scripture passage under consideration. What is God saying through this passage? The amount of time the teacher will give to the matter of understanding the meaning will depend upon the aim the teacher has in mind for the lesson.

Second, the teacher will seek to lead the class to understand more clearly the general Christian principle upon which his aim is based. If his aim is some specific response based on the principle "Love thy neighbor as thyself," then the meaning of this principle must be made clear. If his aim is based upon the Christian ideal of stewardship, or of forgiveness, or the Christian ideal in human relations, it is necessary for the class to understand what is meant by and involved in the ideal.

Third, he will seek to lead the class to a deeper acceptance of and commitment to this Christian ideal. If the teacher is seeking a conduct response in the lives of the members, this response must grow out of their commitment to the ideal. If the response the teacher is seeking calls for change in the lives of the members, they often will not change unless their commitment is deep. There are many Christians who know they ought to do certain things but their commitment in these areas is not sufficiently deep to cause them to change.

Biblical content to be used.—The teacher will recognize immediately that to secure changes in life is neither a simple nor

38

an easy undertaking. The biblical content to be used in the development of the lesson must be in line with the purpose. The question of what biblical content to be used usually arises. The obvious answer is that content which is given in the Scripture passage. But what part of this content will be used and what will have to be left out? What will be emphasized and what will not? To answer these questions the teacher must remember that he teaches the whole lesson for the purpose of achieving his lesson aim. Therefore the development of the lesson must contribute to the achieving of the aim. The aim of the lesson determines what is included in the discussion and what is omitted. What the teacher leaves out of his development is often as important as what he keeps.

Many teachers seem to feel compelled to cover all the material given in the lesson helps. If the aim is a specific conduct response aim, it is not possible to cover all the material. The teacher should include only that which will contribute to the acceptance of the lesson aim and omit all the rest. This means that the teacher will not be able to bring out all the truths contained in a particular passage. It is better for the teacher to seek to lead his class to understand, accept, and live by one truth than to expose them to a number of truths. The teacher must learn to be specific in his teaching.

Arrangement of content.—The material the teacher uses in the development of his lesson, the biblical content and the points to be emphasized, should be psychologically rather than logically arranged.[1] That is, they should be arranged in terms of the learner rather than in terms of the content. The teacher should arrange the material so that it will best contribute to the achieving of the lesson aim rather than so that he will have a logical coverage of material. For example, a recent lesson in the

---

[1] This is true when the teacher has a conduct response aim for the lesson. When he has a knowledge aim for the lesson, the emphasis is on an understanding and mastery of Bible content, and the arrangement will be more logical.

Uniform Series was entitled "Ruth, a Foreigner Who Found a Welcome." The printed Scripture passage was Ruth 2:8–13 and 4:13, 17. This outline was given:

1. A Gracious Gentleman, 2:8–9
2. A Grateful Stranger, 2:10
3. A Generous Attitude, 2:11–12
4. A Gentle Request, 2:13
5. A Glorious Harvest, 4:13, 17

This may be an excellent and logical outline of the biblical content, but it may not at all lead to the achievement of the teacher's aim. A particular teacher, who will know what his aim is, must arrange his development so that it will lead to the achievement of this aim. Sometimes he may want to use the last verse in the passage first. At other times he may want to emphasize two or three verses, omitting the rest. Still again he may want to use one or two verses in the printed passage and then go to other parts of the Bible for scriptures that will lead to the achievement of his aim. The teacher must remember that content is a means to an end. The lesson aim is the end which the teacher is seeking. Therefore the content must be arranged in such a way that the aim will be achieved.

Methods.—The teacher must not only be concerned about the content he is to use and the arrangement of this content, but he must also be concerned about the most effective way or ways to share these ideas and insights with the members of his class. This brings up the problem of method. Of course methods of teaching must also be considered as the teacher prepares the other parts of the lesson. It is mentioned here for the sake of emphasis. Again the teacher's aim for the lesson is the determining factor. How shall the teacher teach so that he will have the best possibility of achieving his purpose? The methods the teacher plans to use are almost as important as the content of the lesson. It is tragic for a teacher to spend a long period of time studying and preparing the content he plans to teach and then give little or no consideration to the most effective methods of using this material.

In developing the lesson the teacher should encourage the active, vocal participation of the members of his class. Too often, teachers have considered their task to be to tell the members what they had learned from their study or to tell what the Bible has to say. This has been a serious weakness in many classes, particularly in Adult classes, and to a lesser extent in classes for Young People, Intermediates, and even Juniors. Good teaching consists in sharing ideas and experiences by both teacher and members. For this reason the teacher must guard against the temptation to do all of the talking during the class period. There should be an active search for the meaning of the biblical material and a sharing of insights and points of view between teacher and pupils and between pupil and pupil. Through this sharing the Holy Spirit may have an opportunity to illumine the understanding of each one in the class, including the teacher.

Making the Lesson Personal

After the teacher has led the class members to understand the basic Christian ideal being considered and after he has sought to lead them to a deeper commitment to this ideal, he must seek to make this ideal personal in terms of their normal, everyday lives. The class should be led to consider how this spiritual truth will affect, or ought to affect, their lives in a specific situation. In the past teachers have tended to teach general principles and, while the members have accepted these general principles, they have not always understood how these principles apply to specific situations in their lives.

The need to make teaching personal applies to Young People and Adults as well as to Juniors and Intermediates. The teacher of a class of adults says, "We need to be more Christian in our business relations." The members already know this, but what, specifically, do they need to do to be more Christian in their

41

business relations? Of course they ought to be honest in their dealings and polite to their customers. But beyond these obvious practices they have difficulty knowing what specifically they should do to be more Christian in their business relations. If you don't believe this is true, try to think of some things yourself! The members need to be led to consider how a general spiritual truth would apply in a specific situation.

How may this be done? One way is to use a "life situation" or, as it is sometimes called, a "what-would-you-do situation." A life situation is a problematic situation involving the spiritual principle being studied. The teacher presents the situation to the class and then asks, "What would you do?" It is a specific situation in which the application of the Christian ideal is difficult to make. To be truly meaningful the life situation must first of all be realistic in terms of the experience of the members. This does not mean that it has to be true. It may be (and usually is) only a hypothetical situation made up by the teacher, but it must be so closely related to the normal experience of the members that they could easily be involved in the situation.

In the second place, the life situation must be one in which conflicting courses of action are open to the members. There are those courses of action that are in line with the normal, human desires of people. Also involved is the more Christian course of action. Third, the life situation must be in line with the teacher's aim. If the teacher's aim is based on the ideal of Christian forgiveness, then the life situation must be one involving the problem of forgiveness. If the teacher's aim is based on the ideal "Love thy neighbor as thyself," then the life situation must be one involving human relations. The idea behind the use of a life situation is that as the members consider the problems in finding and following the Christian course of action in this specific situation, they come to see more clearly how the general spiritual ideal relates to their personal lives.

Using a life situation is only one more or less dramatic way to make the lesson personal. There are other more simple ways.

The teacher may ask, "What are some situations in which this spiritual truth would apply in your lives?" "What are some areas in which we fail to express this truth?" Here, as in all of his teaching, the teacher must have variety in order to hold the interest of the class.

Securing Carry-over

This is one of the most important parts of the entire lesson. Up to this point in the lesson the members have been discussing what *might* be done or what *ought* to be done. In this portion they are led to decide what they actually are going to *do* to express the Christian ideal being considered. This section makes the difference between a lesson that ends in talk and one that leads to action.

The teacher will have carry-over as a part of his lesson plan only when he has a conduct response aim. It is at the point of carry-over that there is a major difference between an inspiration lesson and a conduct response lesson. The inspiration lesson deals with the deepening of some attitude and does not call for a definite response in action. For example, the inspiration aim, "To lead my class members to a deeper faith through a study of the resurrection of Jesus," does not call for a carry-over as a part of the lesson because no specific response is sought. But the conduct response aim, "To lead my class to engage in definite Christian witnessing by speaking to one unsaved person this week," would demand carry-over as a part of the lesson because a definite response is sought.

The teacher's plans.—Too often teachers do not get desired results from their teaching because they conclude the lesson with a general exhortation to the class: "Let's all do thus and so." Experience has proved that this type of exhortation does not often secure the desired response in the lives of the members. Something more definite and specific is needed.

Carry-over involves three things. First, it involves a decision to *want* to do something. Second, it involves a decision as to *what* to do. Third, it involves making necessary plans to carry out the response the members have chosen.

These three steps must be carefully planned by the teacher as he prepares his lesson. It is true that these plans may be changed by the members in the actual class session. They may decide on things the teacher has not planned, but this advance planning will help the teacher regardless of what the class chooses. He should consider how he can encourage the class to make a decision to actually *do* something to express in their lives the spiritual truth they are considering. How can he help them as they are considering what expression they can make? What possible responses could they make? The teacher should seek to forecast these in advance. What plans will be necessary for the members to make if they choose certain responses? How can I help them here? The teacher will have a much better chance of securing response in the life of his members if plans such as these are made than if he simply leaves the matter to chance.

The members' suggestions.—Although the teacher should make careful plans for carry-over, the members must be left entirely free to make their own suggestions. Religion is an intensely personal matter. Therefore, in seeking to lead his members to express their religion in life, there are two matters the teacher ought to keep clearly in mind. First, the response must be freely chosen by the member himself. That is, the response must be the free expression of his own decision, his own desire, and his own commitment to Jesus Christ. The response should not be made simply to please the teacher. Second, and closely related to the first, the response must be based upon a spiritual motivation. Based upon any other type of motivation the response will be merely pharisaical in nature. In the class session the members may be led in general according to the following stages: I have committed myself wholly and unreservedly to Jesus Christ as the Master of my life. This Christian ideal we are discussing is a part of the Christian way of life. I

44

see now that here is a response I ought to make—which I have not been making—as an expression of my commitment to Jesus and to his cause.

There are two things which the teacher must always avoid in seeking to lead his class to make a response. First, he should never put any external pressure upon the class as a whole or upon the members as individuals. Second, he must take care never to embarrass anyone. And his attitude, his interest, his concern, and his love for the members who do not make a response must be just as great as for those who do make a response. If anything, it should be greater for the ones who make no response, for it may be that these are the ones who most need help.

Types of carry-over.—The carry-over sought by the teacher or chosen by the members will be as varied as the Christian life itself. It is limited only by the insight of the teacher and the class members. The criticism is sometimes made that the carry-over by the class is rather shallow and superficial. If this is true, it is true only because the teacher and the members do not see the deeper ways of expressing the Christian faith. The carry-over plan may be quite simple—such as leading the members to start reading the Bible every day. All necessary plans for carrying out the response may be completed quickly and easily in the class session. The response chosen may be more complex in nature and take a period of time to carry out—such as attempting to eliminate some evil in society. It may be so complex that necessary plans for carrying it out cannot be completed in class, and meetings outside of class may need to be held.

There may be responses in which the class will engage in a project as a group. The carry-over may be one in which the class members will choose to engage in the same activity but they will do it as individuals—such as starting a family altar. There may be the type of carry-over in which the members choose different responses according to the need of each individual.

Follow-up by the teacher.—The teacher needs some plan of follow-up to find out whether his teaching is really influencing the lives of his members or not. This is necessary for two reasons. First, he does this not because he wants to spy on his members but because he is genuinely interested in their spiritual growth. He is not content to leave his teaching with only a vague hope that he is doing some good. If the task of teaching is as important as the teacher says it is, he must not leave the results of his teaching to chance. Second, some plan for follow-up needs to be made to let the members know that the teacher really expects them to do something about what is taught on Sunday morning.

Teacher after teacher has reported that when they sought a specific conduct response in a given lesson and the following Sunday sought to check on the response, they found that the members had forgotten to do anything about it and actually seemed surprised that the teacher really expected them to do something. This points to a serious weakness in much of the teaching that is done in the modern Sunday school. Seemingly the members believe that they are not expected to express in any definite and specific way that which they study on Sunday morning. They expect to come, sit, listen, and agree with what is said, but seemingly they do not expect to express any response. Merely listening is, of course, much easier than expressing a Christian commitment in action.

The plan the teacher uses for follow-up will be determined by the type of response desired and by the age group of the class. If the response is in the form of a project the teacher may observe the members at work. With Juniors the teacher may engage in informal talk with the members as they arrive in the class on Sunday morning. With others he may have a report in class. In still other cases he may have a personal conversation with the members during the week. Again, the teacher must take every precaution to avoid embarrassing anyone. Even in the follow-up his purpose is to teach and help the member grow. But he should also let the member understand that he does expect the Christian faith to be expressed in life—not just talked about on Sunday morning.

Thus, it may be that planning for carry-over is the key to the success of a conduct response lesson. The decisions that are made or not made and the plans that are made or not made are pivotal in the effectiveness of the lesson. The teacher must plan this part of the lesson with care.

Guidance in Lesson Preparation

The following questions are given for the guidance of both the department superintendent and the teachers as together they seek to apply these techniques in the preparation of the lesson.

1. Remember to apply that which was studied in the last chapter.

(1) What is the quarter aim? The unit aim?

(2) What is the lesson aim?

(3) Is it intended to be a knowledge, inspiration, or conduct response aim?

(4) Is it brief? Clear? Specific?

2. How will the teacher introduce the lesson to secure a purposeful study of the Bible?

(1) Is the introduction in line with the interest of the class?

(2) Is a vocal response sought from the class?

(3) Is there a transition that leads the class to the Bible?

(4) What will the teacher tell the class to look for as the Bible is read?

(5) Will the discussion of these matters lead naturally into the development of the lesson?

3. What major points will the teacher use in developing the lesson?

(1) Are these points arranged logically (in terms of the material) or psychologically (in terms of the needs of the members and the aim of the lesson)?

(2) Does the development lead the class to a clearer understanding of the Christian truth being studied?

(3) Does the development lead to a deeper commitment to the Christian truth being studied?

(4) What methods will be used in developing the lesson?

4. How is the spiritual truth being studied to be made personal for the members?

(1) How will the teacher seek to lead the members to face specific situations where this truth would apply?

(2) What are some problems the members might have in applying the truth?

(3) How will the teacher seek to lead the members to face seriously the meaning of this Christian truth in their personal lives?

5. How does the teacher plan to secure carry-over?

(1) How will the teacher seek to lead the class to decide to make a response?

(2) How will he seek to lead the class members to decide what response they desire to make?

(3) What plans will the members need to make in order to carry out their chosen response?

(4) What will the teacher plan as a follow-up to determine what response the members make?

4. Teaching to Increase Knowledge

WHEN THE SUNDAY SCHOOL was started, it was not primarily religious in nature. It began outside the church, and its purpose was simply to keep underprivileged children off the streets and to teach them to read and write. However, the book that was studied in the Sunday school was the Bible. Later, when the Sunday school was brought into the churches, leaders saw in this movement a marvelous opportunity to teach both denominational distinctives and the Bible. So great was this emphasis on teaching the Bible that there was a time when the term "Bible school" became rather widespread. In many of the evangelical denominations the Bible has been the central textbook through the years. One outstanding leader in the field has said, "The avowed purpose of the Sunday school is to teach the Bible." With this emphasis on the Bible and Bible study it is reasonable to ask to what extent the Sunday school has been successful in giving to those who attend a real knowledge of the Bible.

Findings of a Bible Knowledge Test

A Bible knowledge test was given in seventeen Baptist churches in the state of Kentucky recently.[1] The questions were purely factual, covering both the Old Testament and the New

---

[1] Russell Bennett, "Measurement of Pupil Bible Knowledge in Selected Baptist Sunday Schools in Kentucky" (Master's thesis, Southern Baptist Theological Seminary, 1957). Used by permission.

Testament. The tests were given in rural and urban churches, and the urban churches were divided according to high, middle, and low income groups. Six hundred and ninety-five returns were received. The average score [2] for the test was 16.57 out of 50, which means that the average grade was slightly over 33 per cent! Sixty-four per cent missed this question: "Jesus said the greatest in the kingdom of heaven would be (a) the servant of all, (b) poor, (c) pure in heart." Sixty-three per cent missed this question: "On the Day of Pentecost 3000 were added to the church after (a) Peter, (b) Paul, (c) John preached." Contrary to prevailing opinion, Adults made a higher score than Juniors and Intermediates. The mean score for Adults was 20.66, for Young People 16.39, for Intermediates 12.64, and for Juniors 5.81. In the urban churches the high income group had a mean score of 32.06, the middle income group 15.39, and the low income group (downtown missions) 1.18. The mean score for all rural churches was higher than the mean score for all urban churches; the rural churches had a score of 17.73 while the urban churches had a score of 15.89. As can readily be seen, the score of the urban churches was brought down by the unusually low score made by the low income group.

The findings of this test are not given as definitive, and, therefore, widespread generalizations should not be drawn. However, these findings do suggest that although the Bible is the central textbook in the Sunday school, there is an amazing lack of knowledge of the Book that is studied. After a person had attended Sunday school for five, ten, fifteen, or more years, studying the same Book week after week, he would be expected to have some mastery of it. Yet such is not the case. And beyond the rather superficial matters that are rather common knowledge such as where Jesus was born and the name of the baby

---

[2] The formula used in determining the score was: $S = R - \dfrac{W}{2}$. The score equals the number of right answers minus the number of wrong answers divided by two. This formula takes into account the factor of guessing.

found in the ark of bulrushes, there is an even more appalling lack of knowledge.

This is not to suggest that a knowledge of the Bible is the ultimate objective of the Sunday school. Of course the ultimate objective of all Christian teaching is that individuals come to know God as Father and Jesus as Saviour and to follow the Christian way. As Smart says, "The purpose of instructing the child in the Scriptures is not just that he may know the Scriptures, but that he may have faith in God as he is revealed in the Scriptures." [3] However, Bible knowledge is a worthy objective. While a knowledge of biblical facts does not necessarily give an accurate measurement of a person's spiritual development, such knowledge does give the individual a basis for a more intelligent Christian faith. For a teacher to seek to lead his members to have a knowledge of the Bible is a worthy objective.

Teaching with a Knowledge Aim

Why is it that people who have attended Sunday school for many years have so little knowledge of the Bible? Undoubtedly there are many reasons. A part of the responsibility (and perhaps a large part) must rest upon the teachers and the way they have taught. Teachers often have taken a short Bible passage and devotionalized about it during the class period. As a result the class members have never developed a logical, systematic grasp of the Bible. This does not mean that it is wrong to teach the Bible devotionally. It does mean that it is wrong to teach the Bible this way *every* Sunday. At times teachers need to teach with a knowledge aim in order to give the class members a systematic comprehension of the Bible.

As was pointed out in chapter two, teachers often try to teach knowledge, give inspiration, and seek conduct response all in the same lesson. In so doing they have not secured adequate

---

[3] James D. Smart, *The Teaching Ministry of the Church* (Philadelphia: The Westminster Press, 1954), pp. 148–49.

results in any one of these areas (unless in inspiration). There are times when the teacher ought to teach with purely a knowledge aim, in which his purpose is to lead his members to have a mastery of some part of the Bible or some aspect of the Christian faith.

Definition and explanation.—A lesson with a knowledge aim is one in which the teacher seeks to guide the class in a serious, systematic study of a significant portion of the Bible leading to an understanding and mastery of the content studied. Each word in the definition is important. First, it is to be a *serious* study, engaged in with purpose. It is not to be a shallow, superficial covering of material. It should be as scholarly as the teacher and the class are able to make it. Second, it is to be a *systematic* study. Whether the group is studying some doctrine or some portion of the Bible, the study should be a logical, systematic consideration of the content. If the study is to lead to understanding, there must be some system to the study. If it is to lead to mastery, there must be some logical organization of the material.

Third, it should be a study covering a *significant* portion of the Bible or some significant aspect of the Christian faith. In other words, if the teacher has a knowledge aim for a lesson he ought to cover more of the Bible than that printed in the quarterly. The basis for his knowledge aim may correspond more closely with what is known as the larger lesson. At times it may include even more than this. The knowledge which is gained by the members through the study of a knowledge aim lesson should be significant both as to content and amount.

Fourth, the study should lead to an *understanding* of the material. This means more than just having the teacher "tell" the class what the meaning is. There must be a grasp of meaning on the part of the class members. This is not a simple matter to achieve.

Fifth, the study should lead to a *mastery* of the knowledge studied. If there is one emphasis that should stand out in a knowledge aim lesson, this is it. The teacher—in planning, in method, in emphasis, in total approach—should seek to lead his members to *master* the material being studied. He should seek to lead them to have such mastery of the content that if they were to be asked a question about it in three months or six months, they would be able to answer. Using this approach in teaching, the teacher would have a far better chance to lead his members to have a knowledge of the Bible than he would if he taught *every* Sunday with the devotional approach.

But does not the teacher use some knowledge when he has a conduct response aim? Surely he does, because response must always be based on knowledge. But the knowledge he uses in a conduct response lesson is that knowledge which will lead to an understanding and acceptance of his conduct response aim. This study may not be a logical, systematic study of a portion of the Bible. The teacher may start the study with one passage, then go quickly to another portion of the Bible, and then to still other parts of the Bible—all seeking to lead the class to an understanding and acceptance of the Christian attitude being studied. But this type of hop, skip, and jump approach to Bible study (perhaps necessary in a conduct response lesson) will not give the members a comprehensive, unified knowledge of the Bible because it does not lead him in a logical, systematic study of the Bible.

Two types of knowledge.—There are two types of knowledge which the teacher may seek to teach. First, there is knowledge as facts. Here the teacher tries to lead his class to master some of the important facts in the Bible, such as the major events in the life of Jesus, the places Paul visited on his three missionary journeys, the events that took place during these journeys, the dates of the letters of Paul, or the events in the early expansion of Christianity. There are certain facts about the Bible which every person who claims to have a knowledge of the Bible ought to know.

Second, there is knowledge as meaning. This second type of

knowledge, of course, is more important than the first, though both are necessary. The teacher usually will have both types in mind when he has a knowledge aim lesson. There will be some facts he will want the class to master. There will also be meaning which he will want the class members to understand and master. If the class is studying the book of Amos, the teacher will want them to know something of the social, economic, political, and spiritual situation in which Amos preached. These are facts that will need to be known. The teacher will also want the class to know the meaning of the message of Amos. The facts serve as the basis for making the meaning clear and accurate.

Quarter, unit, or lesson.—There are times when the teacher will want to have a knowledge aim for an entire quarter. For example, an Intermediate or an Adult class may have the life of Jesus as the basis of their study for a given quarter. The teacher's aim for the quarter might be "To lead my class to master the major events and understand the major teachings in the ministry of Jesus." The teacher will have to make specific what is to be included in "major events" and "major teachings" as everything cannot be included in the quarter's study. In this approach, every lesson during the quarter will be taught with a knowledge aim designed to give the members a mastery of these events and teachings such as they have never had before.

There will be other times when the teacher will want to have a knowledge aim for a unit of lessons. He may not want to teach knowledge for the entire quarter but may have a series of lessons that deal with an area where the greatest need of the class is knowledge. Thus the lessons in one unit may be taught with a knowledge aim while the remaining lessons in the quarter may be taught with inspiration and conduct response aims. Then, there may be times when the teacher will want to have a knowledge aim for a single lesson. In the course of study for the quarter the class may come to a lesson where the teacher feels that the greatest need is for knowledge.

Factors Involved in Teaching Knowledge

Since many Sunday school teachers have never taught a lesson specifically designed to lead the class to a mastery of knowledge, a few suggestions may be in order.

The teacher's knowledge.—The teacher himself must have an understanding and some mastery of the material to be taught. No doubt this is one of the major reasons teachers have not led their classes in a serious, systematic study of the Bible. They do not have the background for such a study. This may be a problem, but it is not an excuse. In an earlier chapter it was pointed out that one of the great needs teachers have is the need for a greater mastery of the Book they teach. Teachers must engage in more serious Bible study. It may be that if a teacher started teaching more lessons using a knowledge aim, he, along with the class, would gain a mastery of the Bible he never had before.

Of course such study will involve work, but all worth-while things involve work. God does not promise an easy way; he does offer a better way. The weekly officers and teachers' meeting can help teachers solve this problem. If, in a given department for a given quarter, all the teachers agree to have a knowledge aim for that quarter's lessons, they can use the weekly teachers' meeting as an opportunity to make a serious, systematic (and as scholarly as possible) study of the Bible content to be taught each Sunday. Such a study of the Bible will enrich their teaching for the rest of their lives.

Background of the class.—The Bible knowledge to be taught must be in line with the members' age and background in the area being studied. A fundamental principle of teaching is that the teacher must build upon the learner's present knowledge. This means that the teacher must know his members well enough to know what their present knowledge is. The material must not be presented so simply as not to stimulate and challenge the members. On the other hand it must not be so difficult that they cannot understand it. The teacher will need to plan parts of the lesson to meet the needs of those who have little background and other parts of the lesson to challenge those with a better background.

Motivation and purpose.—The teacher must motivate the members to have an interest in the material being studied. Without this, little or no learning will take place. Lack of motivation is one of the reasons teachers of Juniors and Intermediates have disciplinary problems. The boys and girls are not "interested" in it; they do not "want" to do it; and they don't "see any sense" in the study. Here are three factors necessary for learning, whether the group being taught is Juniors or Adults —interest, desire ("want"), and purpose ("see any sense"). It is the task of the teacher to stimulate this interest, arouse this desire, and develop this purpose. Let it be clearly understood that it must be the *learner's* interest, desire, and purpose. The teacher may be deeply interested in the study. He may see clearly the purpose of the study. But if the study is to be meaningful and have a lasting effect, it must be the *pupil's* purpose. The study must "make sense" to him.

Organization.—In planning and in teaching the teacher must have his lesson material carefully organized to enable the members to grasp and remember it.

Review.—In teaching knowledge the teacher should review often. This is necessary to make sure the class has grasped and understood what has been covered. Repetition helps the class to master the material.

Variety of method.—In leading the class to a mastery of the material being studied, the teacher will want to use a variety of methods. At times he will ask and answer questions; at other times he will lead a discussion of a specific point. He will use visual aids—slides, filmstrips, maps, chalkboard, or charts—to give information needed by the class. There will also be times when he will lecture. From his own preparation he will have secured information which the class needs and which can best be given in lecture form. However, only rarely will he lecture for the entire class period. The method or methods used will be chosen on the basis of what will best achieve his purpose— understanding and mastery of the material being studied.

New ideas.—New ideas should not be presented too rapidly. To do so tends to blot out those that have preceded. Rather than expose the class to a large amount of material, teachers ought to lead them to master a smaller amount of material.

Steps in Planning a Lesson

A lesson plan for a conduct response aim was suggested in the previous chapters. But when the teacher desires to teach knowledge, his approach to teaching is different; therefore, his lesson plan must be different. The following plan is suggested.

Interest.—As in all teaching, the teacher must begin the lesson in a manner that will stimulate interest on the part of the class members. This means that the teacher must plan some means of motivating his class to want to study and to have some mastery of the portion of the Bible being studied. When the member (be he a Junior or Adult) asks silently, "Why should I study this?" the teacher must have an answer for him. This is simply another way of saying that if learning is to be effective, the learner must have some purpose for the study.

Over-view.—Early in the lesson the teacher may want to give the class an over-view of the study to be made in order that they might have a basis for proper perspective. The members need to see clearly where they are going. This is particularly true if the study of knowledge is to extend over several Sundays and cover a major portion of the Bible. For example, if the class is to spend a number of Sundays studying early Hebrew history, on the first Sunday the teacher might want to lead the class to "peg down" the pivotal points around which the study is to be built. With a broad outline of history clearly in mind, the members will be better able to relate the details of the study to the proper place in this outline.

This division of the lesson might have been called "over-view and review" because Sunday by Sunday, as the teacher leads the class to keep this broad outline clearly in mind, he could also lead them in a review of the material that had been covered in previous lessons.

If a particular lesson on a given Sunday will involve a consideration of a rather complex topic, an over-view of that one lesson will enable the class to see more clearly where they are going. This, again, will help them see how the details fit into the total perspective.

Organization.—This corresponds to the development of the lesson. This portion of the lesson is important because here is the material the teacher wants the class to learn. The arrangement of the material in this part of the lesson must be both clear and logical. The teacher wants to lead the class to have an understanding of the meaning of the portion of the Bible being studied. It is a knowledge of the Bible the teacher is seeking. He wants to lead to a mastery of this knowledge; therefore, the knowledge to be mastered must be carefully organized. The major points to be remembered must be carefully emphasized. It is important that the teacher make sure that this knowledge is organized in the mind of the learner, not just in the notes of the teacher.

Summary and review.—This section furnishes the capstone for a lesson designed to teach knowledge. At the close of the lesson as the teacher leads the class to summarize what has been studied, he seeks to make sure that they have an understanding of the meaning of the material. Points that may still be hazy in the mind of a member are cleared up. The major points are reviewed and organized in a neat package to help the members make this information a part of their permanent fund of knowledge.

Assignment.—The type of assignment given to the class will depend upon the lesson aim the teacher has in mind. If his aim is a conduct response, the assignment may be activity involved in carrying out some project selected by the class. If the teacher has a knowledge aim, the assignment may be to lead the class to look up some information that will be needed for the lesson for next Sunday. Whatever its purpose and however it is done, the assignment must be based upon the interest of the class. Otherwise the members will do nothing about the assignment. Also, if an assignment is made, the teacher must make sure a report is called for on the following Sunday. It is very poor practice for the teacher to make an assignment and never refer to it again. The members will soon learn that the assignment is merely a form the teacher uses and that it really has no meaning for him.

Project.—When the teacher has a knowledge aim for several Sundays (or for a quarter), he may want to lead the class to engage in a project. When this is done, the assignments made will relate to the project. A project usually is an activity engaged in outside of class (though some of it may be done in class). The project should be designed to deepen the pupil's mastery of the material being studied. For example, if the class is studying early Hebrew history, or the period of the eighth century prophets, the members may want to make a chart showing dates, significant political and social conditions, the Hebrew rulers, and the prophets and their messages. Or the class may want to make a notebook of words, places, and people with which they are not familiar.

A Lesson Plan

In the preceding chapter a lesson plan to be used with a lesson using a conduct response aim was given. The following is a lesson plan that may be used with a lesson having a knowledge aim. These lesson plans may be mimeographed and distributed on Wednesday night during the weekly officers and teachers' meeting. The teacher may select one (depending on the type of lesson he plans to teach) and fill it out as he plans his lesson.

Lesson Plan for Knowledge Aim Lesson

1. Aim for quarter:
   (4 spaces)
2. Aim for unit:
   (4 spaces)
3. Aim for lesson:
   (4 spaces)
4. Begin with interest: (to stimulate desire and to give purpose)
   (6 spaces)
5. Over-view: (if needed to give members proper perspective)
   (6 spaces)
6. Organization: (material to be carefully and clearly organized)
   (14 spaces)
7. Summary and review: (to deepen understanding and mastery)
   (10 spaces)
8. Assignment and project:
   (remainder of page)

The Place of Review

Since the purpose of a knowledge aim lesson is to lead to understanding and mastery of content, review is absolutely essential.

Definition of review.—A review is the re-viewing of (taking another look at) material previously covered for the purpose of deepening understanding, seeing new meaning, and achieving mastery. The review must be carefully planned and must be interesting and meaningful to the members; otherwise the teacher may have disciplinary problems, particularly with younger groups. The review should involve all the members. Often when the teacher leads the class in a review, the bright pupils dominate and answer all the questions. Others, who probably need the review most, are left out. How can the teacher make the review interesting and meaningful to all the members? That is a difficult problem and the teacher must make careful preparation for the review.

The function of review.—A review may serve a variety of purposes. On occasions the teacher may want to emphasize one purpose; on other occasions he may want to emphasize another purpose. Generally he will have a variety of purposes in mind.

(1) A review may help the members organize the material they have covered. As has already been stated, if the members are going to master the material and make it a part of their permanent possession, the material must be organized in their minds so clearly that they can carry it away with them.

(2) A review may enable the members to see proper relationships within this particular area and to see relationships between this knowledge and other areas of knowledge. For example, if the group is studying the conversion experience, they may be led to see the relationship between a regenerate church membership and the priesthood of believers. Or they may be led to see relationships between this knowledge and the responsibility of parents to teach children in the home.

(3) A review may serve the purpose of repetition to aid the members in remembering what they have studied. Repetition is a fundamental principle of learning. The good teacher is aware that exposing the class one time to information to be learned does not guarantee their learning it. Therefore he provides a review to help the members fix more firmly in mind the material that has been studied.

(4) A review may serve as a preparation or foundation for learning new material. If the teacher is leading the class in a study that covers several Sundays, he will want to make sure that the class has mastered the material that has been covered before beginning a study of new material. New material must be learned in terms of and be built upon knowledge which has already been mastered.

(5) A review may clarify points that may have been misunderstood. There may be matters that are not quite clear to

some members of the class; other members may have mistaken ideas about certain points. However, as the teacher leads the class to take another look at the material that was studied, he has an opportunity to clear up any mistaken or hazy ideas.

(6) The teacher may use the review to test the amount of learning which has taken place in the class. Of course this procedure gives only a rough evaluation, but it can be a helpful tool for the teacher.

When to review.—Since review is so important in leading the members to an understanding and mastery of knowledge, when should the teacher review? There is no set rule to follow. A review ought to be held when it is needed by the class.

(1) The teacher may review near the beginning of the lesson. This review will cover the material that has been studied the previous Sunday or Sundays. Notice that it is suggested that this be done near the beginning and not at the beginning of the lesson. For the teacher to begin the lesson every Sunday by asking, "What did we study last Sunday?" is not the most effective way to secure the interest of the class. Rather, the teacher should begin the lesson with something that will be of interest to the class, with something that will get their attention and give them purpose, and then lead into a review of what has been studied the previous Sundays. Such a procedure makes the review a meaningful part of the lesson.

In this connection there is a very practical problem the Sunday school teacher faces. His class meets only once a week. It is quite easy for the members to forget in the six days that intervene between class sessions what has been studied. This makes review all the more imperative. It also suggests the importance of the teacher's providing meaningful assignments to stimulate study by the members during the week. This study during the week serves to help the members review the material already studied and leads them to a study of new materials.

(2) The teacher may review briefly within the lesson as various points or areas are covered. After a particular segment

of the lesson has been covered, particularly if it has been a rather complex study, the teacher may say, "Let's summarize what we have just studied," or "Let's review briefly the material we have just covered." This helps the members to organize and crystallize the material as they go along.

(3) He may summarize or review at the end of the lesson. When the teacher has a knowledge aim, he will want to do this in almost every lesson. It is here that the teacher seeks to lead the class to make the material they have studied their permanent possession.

(4) The teacher may lead the class in a more comprehensive review after a relatively large body of content has been covered. This may be done after the class has engaged in a study of a unit that lasts several Sundays.

(5) He may have a still more comprehensive review at the end of the quarter covering all the material that has been studied during the quarter. This review may take most, if not all, of the class period. Therefore the teacher should have covered the content of this lesson in the preceding lesson. In such a review the teacher can get a fairly good idea of what knowledge has been mastered by his members. If the members can recall the material they have studied during the past three months, they have a fair degree of mastery.

In this review the teacher will find that many of the details the class has studied have been forgotten. This is to be expected. In fact the purpose of the details was to make the key ideas meaningful for the members. When this purpose has been achieved, it is no longer necessary to clutter up the mind with needless details.

The Place of Drill

Definition.—Drill is not the same as review and should not be confused with it. Drill is intensive repetition of details to insure swift, accurate response. As the child needs drill in learning the multiplication tables, there are also certain types of Bible

63

knowledge where drill is needed. However a word of caution needs to be given.

When to use.—Drill is needed only for that knowledge for which automatic response is desired—like the automatic response that three times seven is twenty-one. This type of knowledge might include learning the books of the Bible, learning certain basic events and places (such as the place of the birth of Jesus), learning to use the concordance, learning to find passages in the Bible, and learning certain memory verses or passages of Scripture.

The teacher wastes time drilling the class on facts that are never needed as automatic responses. The temptation of the teacher is to drill the class on material for which the class sees no purpose and for which they have no need. The matters to be learned by drill should be carefully selected by the teacher, and the class should be led to see the value of and the reason for learning these facts. Otherwise, because of the monotony of a drill, the members may become disinterested and restless and may create a disciplinary problem. The teacher should select only an absolute minimum number of concepts or facts for drill.

How to use.—It is the task of the teacher to make the drill as enjoyable as possible. In other words, the teacher should provide a setting for the drill that reduces monotony. Ingenious devices have been used to make the drill in learning the books of the Bible interesting and enjoyable. The Sword Drill in the Training Union has been a most effective means to lead people to become adept at finding passages in the Bible. Games, such as "Bible Baseball," may be used in drilling the class on Bible facts. Drills should be spaced properly. Shorter periods of drill, held more often, are better than longer periods held at longer intervals.

Guidance in Lesson Preparation

The following questions will guide the superintendent and teachers in their lesson preparation.

1. Lead the teachers to look at the lessons that are to be taught during the quarter. Do they want to use a knowledge aim for the entire quarter? For the next unit? For the next lesson?

2. Lead the teachers to write out their knowledge aim for the quarter, unit, or lesson. What Scripture passage is to be studied? Is this a significant portion of Scripture?

3. Does the teacher have some mastery in the area to be taught? Does he need further study?

4. How will the teacher begin the lesson? How will he lead the class to want to master this knowledge?

5. Shall he give the class an over-view of the material to be studied? If so, how?

6. How will he organize the material to be learned?

(1) What major ideas does he want mastered? How will he lead the class to engage in a serious study leading to understanding and mastery?

(2) What methods will he use in teaching?

(3) How will he help the class members to organize the material clearly in their own minds?

7. How will he lead the class in a meaningful summary and review of the material studied?

8. What assignment will he make for the class to work on during the week?

(1) Is the assignment meaningful to the members?

(2) Will it help them review the material already studied?

(3) Will it help them learn new material?

9. Will the lesson as planned lead the members to increase their understanding and mastery of Bible knowledge?

Unit II

Helping the Teacher Use a Variety of Methods

5. *Introduction to Method*

"COME IN, Mrs. Lyden! I am so glad you dropped in! Since you teach a class of the same age that I do, perhaps you can help me." The two ladies sat down on the sofa in the living room.

"What do you mean, Mrs. Hill? How could I help you?"

"I have been trying to determine what method or methods would be best for me to use in teaching the Sunday school lesson for next Sunday."

"Why, Mrs. Hill, today is only Monday. I haven't looked at my lesson yet. Anyway, I don't bother with what method to use. I just study the *Teacher* and tell my class what it says."

This is a make-believe conversation, but do you know any place where it might have happened?

Concern About Method

Perhaps you are thinking, "Well, I'm not as bad as the lady just mentioned, but in my teaching I really don't give much attention to the matter of method. After all, I don't see any reason for all this concern about method." In seeking to teach, or more appropriately, in seeking to help another to learn, there are at least three major matters that must be taken into consideration by the teacher. First, after the Bible and all lesson helps have been studied, the teacher must determine first what learning he wants to take place and second what material he will use in order to help this learning to take place. During the week the teacher may spend several hours studying materials which are

69

related to the lesson. He discovers ideas which are meaningful to him and which seem relevant to his objective for the lesson. He may spend considerable time in mastering and organizing this content.

However, it is at this point that the teacher may make one of the mistakes most common among Sunday school teachers· to feel that all that is necessary for him to do in order to teach is to study the material in the lesson and then "tell" the class what he has studied. The teacher forgets that he did not learn the material by having someone "tell" it to him. He learned it through study, through research. He meditated upon it; he analyzed it. In other words, he learned it in the crucible of experience. The members of the class must learn it in a similar way. How can he, the teacher, lead the class to discover the insights and information and develop the attitudes that are in harmony with his objectives? This is where the choice of method is involved in the teacher's preparation.

There is a third problem which the teacher must solve. What is the best way to use his material so that learning may take place? Teachers may ignore method in presenting the lesson, but as a result, too often the members do not "learn" even after the teacher has presented the material. If the purpose of teaching is to help people to learn, then the teacher *must* be concerned with how he can teach so that learning will take place. The teacher must not only know the material in the lesson, but he must also know the best way to *use* this material.

The teacher needs to remember that the members have not done the advance study he has done and thus are not as ready for learning as he is. The teacher must bridge the gap between his study and the pupil's learning. As someone has said, he must forget that he knows and remember only that his pupils do not know. It is not enough for the teacher to know the material; he must also know how to help his learners to know, to feel, to believe, to act. To do this it is imperative that the teacher be concerned about method in teaching.

The Broader Problem of Method

The problem of method involves more than the choice of specific methods. Mr. Baxter was teaching a class of thirteen-year-old boys a lesson on "The Wilderness Wanderings." For ten minutes he had been giving in rather meticulous detail the laws and requirements relating to the ceremonial observances of the Jews. The boys were restless. The class burst into bedlam when one of the boys pulled the chair out from under his neighbor. The teacher stormed out of the room, hurried to the office of the Sunday school superintendent, and defiantly announced, "I quit! I just can't teach those little demons!" After some discussion the superintendent asked, "What were you doing to hold their interest?" "Hold their interest?" Mr. Baxter asked. "I was trying to teach them the Bible, and when someone is trying to teach them the Bible, they ought to be interested!"

This illustration suggests that a part of the problem of method in teaching is seeking to stimulate a desire for learning. For a teacher to say "they ought to be interested" is to miss the point entirely. Whether they ought to be or not is beside the point. The fundamental question is whether or not they are interested. If they are not, it is the task of the teacher to seek to arouse this interest. Otherwise the teacher will have an almost impossible task on his hands.

Closely related to motive is purpose. The pupil inevitably (though perhaps silently) asks himself the question, "Why should I study this?" Why should he study about Moses' leading the Children of Israel out of Egypt? Why should he study about Abraham's journey to the Land of Promise? A part of the broader problem of method (when method is viewed as helping learning to take place) is the problem of leading the members to see purpose in the study. Without purpose—and this must be the learner's purpose—little learning will take place.

Another closely related factor is meaning. The study must have meaning for the learner; it must "make sense" to him.

71

Otherwise he will say (again, silently), "This doesn't make sense to me." And when a study doesn't "make sense," disciplinary problems follow. Thus method is concerned with the following questions which the teacher *must* answer in preparing to teach:

1. How can I help my class develop an interest in this study?
2. How can I help my class develop a purpose for this study?
3. How can I help my class to see meaning in this study?

Choosing a Method

In general there are five methods of teaching: question and answer, discussion, lecture, story, and project. Visual aids is sometimes included in a list of methods. However, the use of visual materials is not so much a method as it is an aid to be used with other methods such as questions and discussions. Role-playing is a relatively new technique which may be included in a discussion of methods.

With this variety of methods available the teacher may often ask, "How will I know which method or methods to use?" There is no "rule" that can be given for the teacher to follow in answering this question. Nor is a "rule" needed. In the average situation no one method is best. For a given lesson, one teacher may use one method. For the same lesson another teacher may use a different method. Both of them may be equally successful so far as learning by the classes is concerned.

However, there are several factors that should be considered in determining which method might be best for a given Sunday.[1] First, the age of the group to be taught would influence the method or methods used. Discussion would be fine for older Intermediates and Young People, but it would be out of place with small children, even if the lesson topic were the same for both groups.

Another factor that should be considered is the aim the teacher has chosen for a given lesson. For example, a lesson may

---

[1] C. B. Eavey, *Principles of Teaching for Christian Teachers.* (Grand Rapids: Zondervan Publishing House, 1940), pp. 237–44.

be entitled, "The Lord's Day in Our Day." One teacher may have as an aim "To help my pupils understand the teaching of the Bible concerning keeping the Lord's Day." Then he might look up all the Bible references, study what the commentaries say, and give a most helpful lecture on what he has learned. On the other hand, another teacher may have as his aim, "To help my pupils discover how to observe the Lord's Day in the day in which we live." Immediately this aim would call for a frank discussion of the problems the class members are facing in light of the teachings of the Bible. This is not to say that one aim or method is better than the other. It does point up the fact that the aim for a given lesson will help determine the method to be used in achieving that objective.

The amount of time available for teaching should also be taken into consideration. One of the advantages of the lecture method is that it is possible for the teacher to present to his class in a relatively brief period material that it has taken the teacher hours to gather. A discussion takes more time. The teacher may not be able to cover as much material, but it is likely that the material which is covered will be better remembered. The project is an effective method, but it also takes time. Some feel that this method, in which the members learn through doing, is so effective they give the entire lesson period to a project. The time for teaching is so brief and so important the teacher must determine what is the most effective way of using that time.

Finally, the background the members have in the area being studied will also have to be considered. If the class is studying in an area of the Bible or Christian truth where they have little or no background knowledge, it would not be wise to try to have a discussion. The members would not have sufficient information to enter intelligently into the discussion. The average adult would not have sufficient background to discuss the social, political, and economic evils of the times of the prophet Amos. But he would certainly have sufficient information to discuss with some intelligence the social, political, and economic evils of his own community.

Many adult teachers complain that their members will not "talk" in class. It may well be that these adults are acutely aware of their limited knowledge in the area of the Bible being studied and seek to keep from revealing their ignorance by keeping silent. This lack of Bible knowledge is a rather severe indictment of the lecture method which teachers have predominantly used in teaching adults. Class members have not learned as much as they should have learned. This is another reason teachers must find and use better methods.

Variety of Method

Which is the best method and which is the worst method? Dr. Gaines S. Dobbins said years ago that the worst method is the method that is used all the time. Regardless of what method it is—discussion, question and answer, or lecture—if it is used Sunday after Sunday with no variation, that is the worst method. I thoroughly enjoy hearing a story. But I would dislike for my teacher to meet the class every Sunday and do nothing but tell a story. Using the same method every Sunday without variation is the worst method.

But which method is best? No one of them is best. Each has its own place and purpose. Probably a combination of two or more methods is best. Here, as elsewhere, variety is the spice of life. A teacher sometimes feels that he should use only one method during the entire lesson period. Of course there will be times when this will be the case. But usually the teacher will use several different methods in a single session. In a given lesson he could use some questions and answers and have some discussion; he might take a few minutes to lecture or to explain a difficult point; he might tell a story. A combination of these methods with the major emphasis now on one and then on another probably is best.

The teacher who has used only one or two methods in his

teaching may feel that he cannot learn to use any other methods. Indeed, many would be frightened by the thought of using a different way of teaching. Nevertheless, with intelligent planning and practice any teacher can improve his use of any method. This does not mean that he will have complete success the first time he tries a new method. The teacher need not be afraid of failure. A boy would never learn to ride a bicycle if he refused to get on it because he was afraid he would fall off. The teacher needs to "get on and ride" with the methods that follow in succeeding chapters.

Method is never an end in itself. It is always a means to an end. The important thing is not that the teacher become proficient in lecturing, asking questions, leading a discussion, or telling a story. The important thing is that learning take place. Will learning be more likely to take place using this particular material, with this particular aim, with this particular class, at this particular time if the teacher lecturers, ask questions, leads a discussion, or if he does some of each of these? Method is simply an instrument used by the teacher to communicate to the learner the knowledge, ideal, or truth under consideration. But just any means will not be adequate. That which is being taught must be communicated to the learner in such a way as to give understanding, to lead to acceptance and conviction, and to secure response. Thus method must always be used in harmony with the principles of learning.

6. Question and Answer Method

THE REASON TEACHERS TEACH is to help others to learn. The wise use of effective questions can be one of the best aids in this process of teaching and learning. Below are listed some of the principles of learning and the way questions can relate to these principles.

(1) Mental activity is essential to learning. Good questions stimulate mental activity on the part of the pupil and may thus lead to learning.

(2) Discovery, that is, leading members to gain new insight, is a vital part of learning. Questions may be used to guide the learner in this process of discovering and thus contribute to learning.

(3) Problem solving is closely related to learning. A question presents a problem to the learner and invites a search for an answer or a solution.

Questions that are carefully chosen and properly used can be great aids in the teaching-learning process. The effective teacher will know how to use the question and answer method with his class.

Types of Questions

There is a tendency on the part of many teachers to use only one type of question. This, of course, makes for monotony in teaching. A teacher would do well to consider the following types and seek to devise questions using these different types in preparing next Sunday's lesson.

Factual questions.—It is probable that teachers use factual questions more than any other type. Such questions are designed primarily to discover what facts or information the pupil may have, or to lead to a mastery of knowledge. This is an entirely worthy and legitimate use of the question. This heading is a general one and may be divided into sub-types.

(1) *Definition.*—This type of question asks a person to use the knowledge he has to define or explain something. Example: What is meant by the word "gospel"?

(2) *Sources.*—This question is concerned with where certain things may be found. Example: Where do you find the most complete account of the birth of Jesus?

(3) *Who, What, When, Where.*—This is probably the most common type of factual question and one of the most important. Example: Who were the Pharisees? What did the Sadducees believe about the resurrection? When did the Jewish Exile start? Where did Jesus make his home after he left Nazareth?

(4) *Classification.*—These questions are designed to lead the members to organize their information or knowledge into some type of classification. Example: List the kings of Southern Israel who were predominantly good and those who were predominantly bad.

(5) *Drill or review.*— These questions help the members fix firmly in their minds information they have studied. Example: Who will repeat for us the books of the Bible?

Thought questions.—These are the questions that are designed to stimulate thought, to seek opinions, and to lead to understanding. Teachers need to give more attention to this type of question, because it has often been neglected. This general category may also be divided into sub-types.

(1) *Stimulate thought.*—There are questions that stimulate the members to think and to share their ideas and opinions with the class. In this way the class may be led to new and deeper insights, one of the prime purposes of teaching. Members will

be heard to say, "I've never thought of it that way before," or "I had not considered that angle of the problem at all." Example: Is it wrong to go to a baseball game on Sunday? Why or why not?

(2) *Deepen understanding.*—Through this type of question the teacher seeks to determine the pupil's understanding in a given area. The questions dealing with understanding are primarily of two types:

a. *Meaning.*—There are those questions aimed at determining whether the member understands the meaning of the Scripture being studied. This is an important type of question because teachers often assume their class members know the meaning of a Scripture passage when they do not. Example: One of the Beatitudes is, "Blessed are the poor in spirit." What does this mean?

b. *Relationship to life.*—This type of question also involves an understanding of meaning but goes one step further. It seeks to determine whether the individual sees any relationship between the passage being studied and his present experience. This is another area of importance where teachers too often assume the members have understanding when, in reality, they do not. Questions seeking to lead the members to indicate their understanding of the relationship of the Bible to their lives should be used often by the teacher. Example: The Bible tells us we should love our enemies. Can you think of any experience in your life where this verse would apply?

(3) *Seek clarification.*—Sometimes the information members have or the ideas they express are rather vague. There are questions a teacher ought to ask to lead a member to clarify his thinking. The purpose of the teacher here is not to challenge the position taken by the pupil but, rather, to help him clarify his thinking to make sure he believes exactly what he has said, or to give him an opportunity to modify his statement. After the person has expressed his idea, the teacher may raise a problem and ask how the person would react to this problem. Example: The

person says, "I believe in the complete separation of church and state." The teacher might then say, "Does this mean that you would not favor having the government support chaplains in the armed forces?"

Stimulating Thought

Since teachers as a rule have had more experience asking factual questions and since they need to be encouraged to give more attention to thought questions, it might be helpful to consider a few specific ways teachers can stimulate thought.

Summarize.—The teacher may ask a member to summarize the class discussion up to that point. This will not only be helpful to the member asked but to the class as well, for too often no specific summarization of ideas is presented, and the discussion of the class ends in vagueness. Example: Mary, will you summarize what the class has been saying up to this point?

Compare.—The teacher may ask a member to compare or contrast. Example: Compare the social conditions in the time of Amos with social conditions in our country today.

General Proposition.—He may give a general proposition and ask the members to give examples. Example: Jesus says we are to love our neighbors as ourselves. Can you give me some examples of things we would do if we carried out this teaching?

Predict consequences.—The teacher may give a situation and ask a member to predict the possible consequences. Example: Johnny is just finishing raking the leaves in his yard in a pile. Jack runs through the pile, kicking the leaves all over the place. If Johnny chases him and hits him, what do you think will happen? What other way or ways can Johnny react? What do you think would happen then? If Johnny were trying to be a peacemaker, what might he do?

Solve problems.—The teacher may lead the individual or group to solve a problem. Example: Sam has been over-spending his allowance in such a way that his parents have told him that they would not advance him his allowance under any circumstances. This week he has spent all his money except twenty cents and the ten cents tithe for the church. Saturday night his best friend calls and asks Sam to go to the show with him. The show costs thirty cents. What can Sam do?

Improving Questions

How can the teacher improve his questions? This question is of prime importance. The following are some simple, practical suggestions that may be of help to the teacher.

Master the material.—Mastering the material is not simple, but it is basic. Many teachers do not ask questions because they are afraid the members, in return, will ask them questions which they cannot answer. These teachers need to realize that one of the first things a good teacher has to learn is to be able to say, "I don't know," without embarrassment. On the other hand, a certain mastery of the material is essential. If the teacher has to spend all his time and mental energy searching for bits of material to fill in the class period, he has little or no time or energy left to plan interesting and different ways of leading the members into insights, meaning, and mastery of the material.

Plan carefully.—During the lesson preparation the teacher ought to plan carefully the questions he is going to use. If the teacher is not in the habit of asking questions in class, he will probably need to write into his lesson plan practically all the questions he wants to ask. After he has become proficient in this area, perhaps he will need to write out only the key questions and let others grow out of the class discussion.

Be clear.—It is obvious that a good question ought to be clear to the class. Again, writing out the questions is good discipline here. Does the question ask exactly what the teacher wants to ask? Is it clear to the members of the class? If the teacher asks a question and then has to repeat it in different words to explain it, it is not a good question.

Be brief.—Questions should not be long and involved. They should be brief enough that the members remember them.

Yes-no questions.—The teacher should guard against the overuse of questions that may be answered with a simple yes or no. This does not mean that these questions should never be used. However, such questions do not have as much "leading on" value to class discussion as do other types of questions.

Use more thought questions.—Or to state the matter negatively, avoid the over-use of factual questions. Factual questions are important and exceedingly valuable. However, observation has indicated that when teachers do ask questions, most often they are factual questions. The suggestion here is that the teacher ought consciously to ask more thought questions.

Time to think.—When the teacher asks a good question, he should give the members time to think before they answer.

Include all members of the class.—This really involves two ideas. First, when a question is asked, it should challenge the attention and thought of each member in the class. This may be done simply by asking the question of the class as a whole before letting someone volunteer the answer or before calling on someone to answer. Example: "Why do you think it is more difficult to live the Christian life today than when our grandparents were children? What do you think, Joe?" rather than, "Joe, why do you think it is more difficult to live the Christian life today than it was when our grandparents were children?" Second, draw shy members in by asking them simple questions.

Planning questions.—The teacher should keep in mind the
(1) Age level and the
(2) Previous knowledge and experience of the members.
The questions should not be so easy as to insult the intelligence of the class or so obvious as to warrant no answer.

No answers.—"I can't get my class to say anything when I ask a question" is a common complaint by many teachers. If this is the situation, the first thing the teacher ought to do is analyze the type of questions he has been asking. It is highly probable that almost all of the questions have been factual. If this is true, it is possible that the class did not respond because they did not know the answer. Perhaps they were not sure of the answer and hesitated to speak out for fear they might be wrong. To remedy this situation, the teacher might try asking more thought questions. He might also seek to devise those questions that will be of real interest to the class members as well as in line with their age level and experience.

Pupil Questions

It is far more important that the teacher answer the pupil's questions than that the pupil answer the teacher's questions.

Stimulating pupil questions.—Some teachers say they can't get their members to ask questions. At least two reasons may lie behind this situation. First, the past experience of the class members in Sunday school may have taught them that they were expected to sit quietly and listen. They have done this so long that it has become a habit with them. If such is the case, the teacher will have to be patient as he seeks to help the members develop a new habit of participating in the class discussion. A second reason may be that the class is not sufficiently interested in what the teacher is teaching to ask questions about it. This indicates that the teaching has not become real to the class members in terms of their life and experience.

In seeking to stimulate questions the teacher sometimes asks, "Do you have any questions about this?" While this may at times provoke a question, most of the time it will not. The teacher should be warned not to depend on this alone.

By far the most effective way of stimulating questions by the members is to make the lesson so real to them, so close to where they live, so related to some of the problems they face that questions will naturally come. This means that both the teaching and the questions of the teacher must be planned carefully in terms of the present life and experience of the members.

Attitude of the teacher.—The attitude of the teacher is important in this matter of stimulating questions by the pupils. The class can detect whether the teacher resents or welcomes questions and will act accordingly. It is not enough for the teacher merely to invite questions. His whole attitude and his approach to teaching must indicate that he welcomes questions; otherwise, the members will sit quietly. The teacher must treat each responsible question with respect and give the time to it that its importance warrants.

Questions off the subject.—Should the teacher answer a question that is off the subject or not? Should he ever leave his lesson entirely? Actually, here is where the art of teaching comes in. There is no rule that can guide the teacher in all situations. However, the following are three questions the teacher ought to consider in determining the amount of time he might use in answering a question that is off the subject. The teacher must answer these test questions in the split second between the time the pupil asks the question and the teacher starts to answer it. It is not so much that the answers are reasoned conclusions; the teacher almost has to feel the answers.

(1) Is the question important to the person asking it? Sometimes a member may burst forth with a question which is unrelated to the lesson but which has been bothering him for a long time. In this question he is revealing a deep seated need. He wants the answer right then, and of course the best time for the teacher to try to answer it is right then. On the other hand, a member may ask a question just to be asking a question. Sometimes a question may be asked simply to try to start an argument about the answer. Or the question may be one that happens to pop into his mind, and he is not seriously concerned about the answer. The teacher must consider whether the question is really serious to the person asking it.

(2) Is the question worthy of serious consideration? The very nature of the question itself will help the teacher know how much time and attention should be given to the answer. Certain questions are quite superficial in nature and need only a superficial answer. However, other questions strike right at the heart of life and religion. The question may be one that is a serious

stumbling block in the individual's Christian understanding and growth. It may be a question that the pupil is facing in his immediate experience, and he is seeking help in trying to find the Christian attitude or course of action.

(3) Is the question of importance to the other members of the class? If the question is so personal that it concerns only the individual asking the question, it may be wise for the teacher to suggest talking privately after class. On the other hand, it may be that one member is raising a question that is of vital concern to the whole class. It may be a theological question that has been raised by a teacher in a high school science class. Or it may be that a matter has arisen in the community, and the members are seeking to find the Christian attitude.

If the answer to all three of these questions is no, the teacher should answer very briefly and come directly back to the lesson. But if the answer to all three of the above questions is yes, the teacher will have to determine how much time should be given to answering the question. There may be times when the question is so important to the members of the class that the lesson for the day might be abandoned and the class led in a search for the answer. Such questions provide a marvelous teaching opportunity. However, it is probable that the times when the teacher would leave the prepared lesson completely would be exceedingly rare. It is far more likely that most of the questions that arise can be answered within the framework of the regular lesson. But it is far more important that the teacher answer the pupil's questions than that the pupil answer the teacher's questions.

Guidance in Lesson Preparation

The superintendent should lead the teachers as they prepare the next Sunday's lesson. It will be helpful for the teachers if he will put the outline of this chapter on the chalkboard. Each teacher will need to note particularly the questions that are planned. Are a sufficient number asked to insure interest and participation on the part of the class?

The superintendent will lead each teacher to analyze and evaluate his questions in terms of the following:

1. How many may be answered by yes or no?
2. Are they brief?
3. Are they clear?
4. Which of the questions are factual?
5. What type of factual questions are being asked? Definition? Sources? Who, What, When, Where? Classification? Drill or review? Other? The teachers need to be sure not to overuse any one type.
6. Which are thought questions?
7. Are these questions primarily to: Stimulate thought? Deepen understanding? Seek clarification?
8. What type of thought questions are being asked? Summarize? Compare? General proposition? Predict consequences? Solve problems? Other? The teachers need to try to use various types.

7. The Discussion Method

THE DISCUSSION METHOD is proving to be one of the most popular and fruitful methods of teaching. People like to talk. This is true of men as well as women, of boys as well as girls. They talk about the weather, politics, crops, the latest styles, hats, sports, and everything else.

Through study of the Bible each Sunday the teacher seeks to help his members solve the problems they face and make their decisions in a more Christian way. But how can he help these members unless he lets them express what they think? The use of the discussion method will give each one an opportunity to share his ideas and experiences. In a good discussion opinions are exchanged, ideas are clarified, attitudes are formed, and decisions are made. In addition, the use of this method will secure the interest of the class as almost nothing else will do. A good discussion can change a dull, dry class session into a lively, sparkling, meaningful experience. The effective teacher will use this method often in his teaching.

The Discussion Method

A discussion is a co-operative search for truth in seeking the solution to a problem. Just because the class members talk does not mean the teacher is employing the discussion method. Unless a problem is involved and unless the group is actively and jointly seeking the solution to a problem through a sharing of ideas and experiences, the teacher is not using the discussion method.

A discussion is not a debate. Sometimes a teacher introduces a problem, but the class, instead of entering into a discussion, engages in a debate. The teacher and the class members should understand clearly the difference between a discussion and a debate; otherwise that which starts out as a discussion may end up as a debate.

What are some differences between a discussion and a debate?

1. A discussion expresses individual views; a debate defends a formal position which has been taken.

2. A discussion seeks new insights; a debate seeks to prove a point.

3. A discussion is a joint search for truth; a debate seeks to win an argument.

4. A discussion presents several alternatives; a debate presents only two.

5. A discussion should never become personal; a debate may.

6. A discussion is concerned with understanding other points of view; a debate is concerned with refuting points that run counter to the position one has taken.

7. A discussion has unlimited participation on the part of the class members; a debate has limited participation.

8. A discussion is informal; a debate is formal. (If debate is informal it becomes an argument.)

A discussion is a joint co-operation on the part of all members of the class in a search for truth. The class may be facing a problem like this: What can we do to make our homes more Christian? The purpose of a discussion in this instance is not to prove a point or win an argument but to get out in the open all relevant facts and insights the class members have for all to see and consider. No one person has all the truth. It is probable that everyone has some of the truth. Therefore it is important that each member participate. In the discussion each individual evaluates the various ideas and points of view as he seeks to come to a conclusion or a decision. This process of evaluation of different points of view is invaluable in Christian teaching. It forms the basis of intelligent decisions, and these decisions tend to grow into attitudes which direct actions and shape lives.

Of course the age group of the class will influence both the nature of the problem and the function of the teacher in a discussion. With Primaries and Juniors the problem will be simple, and the time given to a discussion relatively brief. The teacher will need to give considerable guidance with these age groups. With Young People and Adults the problems become more complex and more time will be needed for an adequate discussion. With older groups more freedom may be given to the class in their discussion.

Factors Involved in a Good Discussion

The problem.—There are several factors necessary to a helpful discussion. First, the class must be confronted with a genuine problem. The word "genuine" is highly important. The teacher cannot expect to get a lively discussion over a matter that presents no problem to the group. It must not be a make-believe problem. It must be a real, live issue that presents alternatives. Some teachers complain that they simply cannot get their members to "discuss." It may be that the teacher is not dealing with issues in religion and life that are really alive for the class members. The teacher must recognize the difference between teacher-interest and pupil-interest. The teacher, because of his study and his background of experience, may be deeply interested in a given problem, but his class members may not be interested in it at all. It may be that the problem is so vital the teacher should seek to arouse the group to an awareness of the problem. But it still stands that until the problem becomes alive for the group, the teacher will have no meaningful discussion.

This suggests a second important consideration. The problem must be *felt* and *accepted* by the group as their problem. Many times it is the task of the teacher to make the class aware of problems in their lives which they have not yet faced or felt.

88

For example, the lesson may be on the topic "Things of Greatest Importance." This topic is simply bursting with opportunities for lively discussion. Do the members of the class *really* believe that spiritual things are of greatest importance? Then what are the implications of this fact for their lives? Here the teacher, through guided discussion, has an opportunity to open the door to many areas in the lives of the class members where Jesus does not have first place. But each member must be led to accept it as his own personal problem before he will enter into a lively discussion. Too much stress cannot be placed upon the nature of the problem to be considered if the teacher plans to use the discussion method.

There are many different types of problems a teacher needs to lead his members to face as he seeks to help them grow in their Christian experience. There is the "what-to-do" type. "What should we do to help the young people of our church?" This type of problem calls not only for discussion but also for action. The teacher has not fully taught if all he does is to lead the class to talk about the problem. If action is called for, action should follow.

There is the "how-to-go-about-it" type. "How can we have more reverence in our worship services?" This type also calls for both discussion and action. There is the "intellectual" type. "Do we believe in the bodily resurrection?" There is the "attitude" type. "What is the Christian attitude toward minority groups?" The teacher will need to know the members of his class so intimately that he will know the problems they are facing. Only in this way can he make his teaching truly personal for his members.

Attitude of the teacher.—A second important factor in any good discussion is the attitude of the teacher. This attitude is not limited to the time the discussion is in progress; it includes the attitude the teacher has displayed in all his previous teaching. The general relationship of the teacher and his class members is most significant.

In using the discussion method, particularly, the teacher should maintain a searching attitude. Discussion is a co-operative search for truth. The teacher is one of these searchers. The teacher must recognize that the members have ideas and experiences that are valuable and should encourage them to share their views and insights with each other. Of course the teacher also has views that are valuable, and he will feel free to share these with the class. Indeed, as teacher, he is under obligation to do so. But as teacher he does not have all the truth nor does he necessarily have the last word.

The teacher should let it be known that he welcomes all points of view even when these views differ from his own. He ought to respect the opinions of his members even when he doesn't agree with them. He should never be shocked at any statement a class member may make. The members must feel that the teacher's interest and understanding are genuine. Blessed is the teacher who has gained the confidence of his class. It is not achieved overnight.

Attitude of the members.—The attitude of the members in a discussion will depend largely on the attitude the teacher has demonstrated in all his previous teaching. Two things need to be noted relative to the attitude of the members in a class discussion. First, they must be willing to state their true attitudes. Many times pupils do not say what they really think; they simply answer as they think the teacher wants them to answer.

Teachers, by their total approach to teaching, ought to encourage their members to be more honest in expressing their real views in Sunday school. But some teachers do not. They want the members to give the "right" answer, and the members know what the "right" answer is and give it. The tragedy is that when these members are faced with a problem in life, they choose their course of action on the basis of what they *really* believe but which they did not express in Sunday school.

Closely related to the attitude of freedom of expression is a second freedom. The individual member must have the freedom to disagree with others, including the teacher, and he must be willing to allow others to disagree with him without becoming upset. Too often the teacher tends to dominate the class to such an extent that if a member dares to disagree with him or with another member, the atmosphere of the class immediately becomes charged with tension. This is indeed unfortunate. All members of the class should feel free to express their views. Only in this way can all points of view be considered.

It is entirely possible to maintain a Christian attitude and spirit in a class session even though members may disagree. Discussion is a co-operative search for truth. Each member ought to seek to understand other points of view. Each should give a fair and objective evaluation to each view that is presented even though it may differ from his own. It is in the back and forth exchange of differing ideas and views that a person really grows in insight. It is through such sharing of ideas that a person may come to a deeper understanding of truth.

Seating arrangement.—Seating arrangement is important in having a good discussion. It would be better for all teaching if the old formal arrangement of seating members in rows were eliminated. Seating the members in rows almost invariably calls for a teacher-dominated class, while seating the class in a circle makes for a much better teaching situation. It is almost a necessity to have the class seated in a circle to create the atmosphere for a lively discussion. This informal seating arrangement makes participation by the members far more natural.

Since a discussion is the sharing of ideas and experiences by all the members, the teacher will want to note the following:

(1) How many of the members participate? In a small class of Junior boys, probably all will take part. In an Adult class with twenty in attendance it may be that not all will make a contribution (though they might). However, the teacher will seek to secure as wide participation as possible.

(2) What proportion of the questions are asked by the teacher? The teacher is the guide of the discussion, and from

time to time he will want to raise pertinent and relevant questions. These are the questions the teacher will want to plan during the lesson preparation period.

(3) What proportion of the questions are asked by the members? If the discussion is truly meaningful to the members, questions will arise in their minds. The more questions raised by the members, the more meaningful the discussion is.

(4) What proportion of the questions are answered by the teacher? At times the members will want to know what the teacher thinks and will direct questions to him. The teacher, of course, is still the teacher even in a discussion and should feel free to participate and share his own views and insights, though he should guard against trying to dominate the discussion.

(5) What proportion of the questions are answered by the members? The teacher is not expected to know all the answers nor is he expected to answer all the questions. Many times questions that are raised by members will be answered by other members. The following diagram will illustrate this back-and-forth sharing between the teacher and members and among the members themselves.

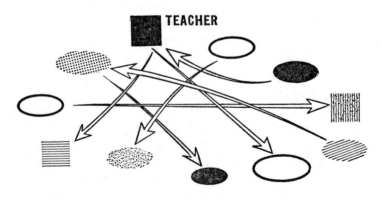

Types of Discussion

It is time now to consider the nature of the discussion itself. What are the essential parts of a discussion? How does one plan for a discussion? In seeking to understand the nature of a discussion the teacher should recognize that there are two types of discussion, though this distinction is not often made.

The structured discussion.—The structured discussion is a relatively formal procedure used to consider a problem of major importance about which there is significant difference of opinion. Note the three factors stated in this sentence. First, it must be a problem of major importance. That is, the problem must be both large in scope and important in terms of the interest of the group. It is probable that a discussion of this type would consume the entire class session. For example, the problem, "Is it wrong to dance?" is a major problem which almost all Intermediates and Young People have to face in one way or another. This problem is large in scope and important to these age groups. Second, it must be a problem about which there is likely to be significant difference of opinion in the group. If there is general agreement concerning the problem, there will be little or no discussion.

In the third place, the structured discussion follows a relatively formal procedure. There are certain prescribed steps which the teacher must observe. These have been variously stated but all are based on John Dewey's statement of the steps in problem solving. The following steps are suggested.

(1) *Statement of the problem.*—Is it wrong for a Christian to dance?

(2) *Definition of the problem.*—Definition may continue throughout the discussion as the group says, "We mean this and not that." However, a definition of words that might be misunderstood or that might mean different things to different people ought to be defined at the beginning of the discussion. What is meant by "dancing"? Does it include any and all types of dancing? Is there a distinction between types—folk dancing, square dancing, supervised ballroom dancing, and dancing at public dance halls? What is meant by "wrong"? Is it morally wrong? Is it wrong in what it may lead to? Is it not morally

wrong for the individual but wrong in the sense that it would hurt his influence?

(3) *Discussion of the issues.*—It is here that the Bible would be studied for an understanding of the Christian principles involved. Here also the members would express their views concerning the problem.

(4) *Possible solutions identified.*—After the problem has been discussed at some length, the teacher (or member whom the teacher asks) will summarize the views that have been expressed and will state the different solutions that have been suggested. This step of summarization and identification of possible solutions is most important; otherwise, the group may continue in a vague, hazy discussion without really pinning down any specific suggestions.

(5) *Possible solutions evaluated.*—Of course this process of evaluation is going on in the minds of the members throughout all the previous discussion as various views are expressed. However, after all the possible solutions have been identified, it is well for the teacher to lead the group in a re-evaluation in light of the total discussion.

(6) *Decision.*—This is the climax of the whole discussion. Decisions should be made in the spirit of worship. Throughout the discussion and particularly in this step the teacher should lead the members to be keenly aware that they are Christian and that they are to make their decision in the light of their total Christian commitment, in the light of their understanding of the Christian gospel, and under the leadership of the Holy Spirit.

Each member must be left completely free in making a decision. The teacher must not use any kind of pressure to force the members to accept his view. If he does, he may get verbal agreement, but the lives of the members will be controlled by their inner decisions which they left unexpressed in class.

At the end of a discussion the teacher ought to lead the group to make a decision. The teacher ought to tie up the loose ends of a discussion in a manner similar to the following: First, if there seems to be general agreement as to the conclusion, the teacher may ask, "Will someone please state our conclusion in the matter?" This statement should be written on the chalkboard to make sure it says exactly what the group wants it to say. Since the group may want to modify this statement to make it more exact, the thinking of the group will be further clarified. Second, if there seems to be differences of opinion among the members, have the different conclusions stated. The teacher may say, "We seem not to be in agreement concerning this matter. Who will state the conclusion of one position?" "Who will state a different position?" These conclusions should be written on the chalkboard. The discipline involved in trying to state a position in a clear and precise manner to be written down is helpful for organizing the thinking of both the individual and the class.

(7) *Action.*—If any action needs to follow the decision that has been made, plans for action will be made by the group. Whether or not there needs to be action will depend upon the kind of problem being discussed. If action is needed, this step, then, becomes the most important of all.

The unstructured discussion.—The unstructured discussion is a consideration of a simple problem or question where there is little possibility of significant difference of opinion. There are three differences between this type of discussion and the one previously presented. First, the problem considered in the unstructured discussion is much more limited in scope. One deals with a major problem; the other deals with a relatively minor problem. Second, the unstructured is much more limited in the amount of time given to it. One may consume the whole class period, while the other may take three or four minutes. Third, the unstructured discussion is much less formal in nature. The steps presented above are not necessarily followed. It is this type of discussion which has been used most often in our Sunday schools. While this type will probably continue to be the most frequently used, it is strongly suggested that teachers try using the structured discussion, following the steps suggested, and giving the whole class period to it.

The Teacher's Function

What is the task and responsibility of the teacher who leads a discussion?

Plan.—He must plan carefully for the discussion as he prepares the lesson. Helpful discussions do not just happen. See pages 100–102 for an example of the type of planning the teacher needs to do.

Pose the problem.—He must pose the problem for the group. In presenting the problem there are three things he must seek to do: first, arouse the interest of the members; second, show the importance of the problem; third, lead the class members to become aware of the relevance of the problem to their lives. The members must become personally involved in the problem before they will enter into a meaningful discussion.

Guide.—The teacher must serve as a guide. It is important that he direct the discussion as follows:

(1) *Keep the discussion "on the track."*—As various views are expressed, it is easy for the group to get off the main problem and engage in aimless talk. It is the responsibility of the teacher to see that this does not happen, and if it does, to bring the group back to the major question before them.

(2) *Lead the group to avoid "blind alleys."*—There are some issues that are fruitless for the class to pursue. The teacher, with his more mature experience, should lead the class to avoid wasting time on these issues.

(3) *Contribute to discussion.*—As teacher and as guide for the discussion he should feel free to express his own opinions and make his own contributions.

(4) *Be careful not to dominate the discussion.*—As teacher, he has a certain status. In some classes when the teacher expresses his view, the class feels that the last word has been

spoken on the matter. The teacher will have to guard against cutting off discussion in this way.

Clarify issues.—The teacher will want the group to see clearly the issues involved in the problem and know what these issues mean.

Give information.—To the extent that it is possible the teacher will have the information the class will need in dealing with the problem. It is not expected that the teacher will know everything, but he should study diligently to have as much information on the subject as possible.

See all sides.—The teacher will want to see that all sides of the question have proper consideration. He will call attention to all relevant information, even that information which supports a position with which he disagrees. He will certainly respect the views expressed by all members of the class.

Allow freedom.—A large amount of freedom must be allowed if the group is to have a good discussion. However, this does not mean unbridled freedom for the class members. Freedom must be balanced with authority. A class does not respect a teacher who, in the name of freedom, lets a class run riot. The age of the class members is important here. More authority will of necessity have to be exercised with Juniors and Intermediates. More freedom will be allowed with Young People and still more with Adults.

Encourage participation.—The teacher will lead as many of the members as possible to participate in the discussion. There may be some in the class who are hesitant to speak. He should plan to draw them into the discussion without embarrassing them. It is not always those who talk the most who have the most to contribute. Often the hesitant or shy individual may have some real insight which he needs to share with the class.

Avoid monopoly.—He should guard against letting one person or a few monopolize the discussion. This may be done without embarrassment. He may simply say, "Thank you,

Mr. ———. Now let's see what some of the others think." All contributions should be brief and to the point.

Conclude the discussion.—The teacher must bring the discussion to a suitable conclusion. There are three things the teacher may do in this connection. First, he ought to have periodic summaries during the discussion to identify the points that have been made. Second, at the end of the class session he may seek a clear statement of the conclusion if there is agreement among the members. Or, third, he may lead them to state their differing conclusions.

Values

The discussion method has numerous values in teaching and learning. A few of these are listed.

1. It leads the members to become aware of and face some of the problems they need to face as Christians. Christianity is concerned with life. Life is filled with problems. Therefore, these problems ought to be a matter of major concern for Christian teachers as they seek to help their members grow in the Christian life.

2. It enables a person to gain new information and deeper insights from the views expressed by fellow class members and the teacher.

3. It gives an individual the opportunity to study the teachings of the Bible in terms of a problem he is facing in life. This will make the Bible and the teachings of the gospel become much more meaningful to him.

4. It gives him an opportunity to express and clarify his own views in the light of the total class discussion.

5. It gives him an opportunity to evaluate and perhaps revise his own views in the light of the total discussion.

Limitations

The discussion method, like any other method, has its limitations, some of which are listed below.

1. A discussion in a class may be merely aimless talk. It may not lead to a positive conclusion, and it may not lead to action when action is needed. However, this is the fault of the teacher and not the method.

2. The group may not have sufficient information to engage in a discussion of a given problem. Discussion without valid information or facts is mere idle prattle.

3. The conclusion may not be correct even though the class agrees on it. The members' agreement does not make it correct. The conclusion they reach may be based upon ignorance and/or prejudice.

4. The time allotted for study may be too brief to consider properly the topic being considered. This is a matter the teacher will have to decide. The time in the class session is precious. On occasion this time may be most profitably spent leading the class in a discussion. On other occasions the time will be better spent using some other method.

5. At the conclusion of the discussion the class may have questions that are still unanswered. In this case the teacher must decide: (1) whether to get more information and spend more time later discussing the problem, or (2) accept the unanswered questions for the time being and pass on to another topic of study. The type of unanswered questions will influence this decision. The teacher will need to decide whether the questions that remain are of deep concern to the group and whether there is a reasonable possibility of finding a satisfactory answer.

Guidance in Lesson Preparation

The time has come now for the teachers to prepare the lesson for Sunday. The superintendent should help them apply what has been learned about the discussion method.

1. Will the teachers seek to lead their classes in a simple discussion or in a more formal, structured discussion?

2. The teachers might also discuss the attitude of their class members as to:

(1) Their willingness to express frankly their views in a discussion.

(2) Their willingness to disagree with other members in the class.

3. The superintendent will lead the teachers to study the lesson and decide what problem they will raise for discussion by the class. Each teacher will write out his statement of a problem. It is usually best for the problem to be stated in the form of a question. Let the teachers, as a group, evaluate each problem they have worked out:

(1) Is it real to the group in terms of their experience?

(2) Is it a problem that is of interest or concern to the class?

4. The teachers will consider the following questions as they continue their lesson preparation.

(1) How does the discussion fit into the teacher's total lesson plan?

(2) How will the teacher introduce the discussion so as to secure the interest of the class and deepen this interest into Christian concern?

(3) How will the Bible be used in this discussion?

(4) What religious principles are involved in this problem?

(5) Does the teacher have questions prepared that will stimulate thought on different sides of the issue?

(6) How does the teacher plan to lead the class to a conclusion?

(7) What will the teacher do if there is a difference of opinion among the members?

Perhaps these examples will help the teacher to see more clearly how to plan to use the discussion method.

Unstructured discussion.—This is a brief, simple discussion. The problem raised by the teacher may be, "What should a Christian do on Sunday?" The members could give their views, which the teacher might write on the chalkboard. He then might ask, "What should a Christian not do on Sunday?" Again the members could express their views. This discussion possibly would take three to five minutes. The teacher would then pass on to another part of the lesson.

However, this same problem could be enlarged, if the teacher so desired, until it became practically a structured discussion, though in the example that follows the various steps are not all followed.

Problem: Should a Christian go to movies on Sunday? The teacher might prepare questions similar to the following to guide the discussion.

(1) What is the teaching of the Bible concerning Sabbath observance?
(2) Could a general principle be stated from this Bible study? Can the class formulate such a principle? Write it on the chalkboard.
(3) Is there anyone who would disagree with this statement or state it differently? Write this on the chalkboard.
(4) Does going to movies on Sunday violate this principle? Why or why not?
(5) Does watching television on Sunday violate this principle? Why or why not?
(6) Can someone summarize what has been said and state what seems to be a conclusion? Write on chalkboard.
(7) Does anyone differ with this conclusion? How would you state it? Write on chalkboard.

Structured discussion.—This is a more formal discussion of a major problem that will take most if not all the class session.

(1) Statement of the problem: Is social drinking bad for the individual and for society?
(2) Problem defined and clarified:
   a. What is meant by "social drinking"?
   b. What is meant by "bad"? Is it wrong religiously? Is it wrong morally? Is it bad in the sense that it hurts one's influence? Are all of these included?
(3) Discussion of issues involved; possible solutions identified; possible solutions evaluated. All three of these steps are included in the following questions:

101

a. What is the teaching of the Bible about drinking? The teacher and members should constantly be relating the discussion that follows to this Bible study.
b. Is social drinking bad all of the time? Why or why not?
c. Is social drinking perfectly acceptable? Why or why not?
d. Is social drinking permissible on certain special occasions? Why or why not?
e. Will someone please summarize what has been said thus far?
f. Is social drinking bad for society but not for the individual? Why or why not?
g. Is social drinking bad for the individual but not for society? Why or why not?
h. What about the individual who says, "It's nobody's business but mine what I do about social drinking"?

(4) Decision—to be made in light of one's understanding of the teaching of the Bible, in light of one's total Christian commitment, and in light of the class discussion.
a. What seems to be our conclusion in this matter? Can we formulate our conclusion in a statement? Write statement on chalkboard.
b. Are there those who would disagree with this statement? How would you state your conclusion? Write on chalkboard.

Evaluating the Discussion Method

Following are questions that will help the teacher evaluate the effectiveness of the discussion method after he has used it.

Tests as to learning.—Animated talk by the members of the class does not mean that they have had an effective discussion or that teaching or learning has taken place. The teacher is not primarily concerned with method but with whether or not his members have learned anything.

(1) Did the members secure information through the discussion they would not otherwise have learned?
(2) Did they confront alternatives they needed to face?
(3) Was their thinking clarified by the discussion?
(4) Have they been encouraged to come to a more intelligent conclusion in light of the discussion?

Tests as to technique.—These questions have to do with the effectiveness of the method itself.

(1) Did all or nearly all of the members actively participate?

(2) Did the members express their true feelings and attitudes?

(3) Did the members ask questions of each other as well as of the teacher?

(4) Did the members direct their remarks to each other as well as to the teacher?

(5) Was there an attitude of a co-operative search for truth through the sharing of ideas?

(6) Did the members listen to each other without interrupting?

(7) Did they seem to take the discussion seriously?

(8) Did the members (and the teacher) respect other people's views even though they disagreed with them?

(9) Did the discussion come to a satisfactory (not necessarily unanimous) conclusion?

(10) Was action needed? Was any taken?

8. The Lecture Method

THE LECTURE METHOD had its origin centuries ago when there were few or no books for the student. It was necessary for the teacher to give to the student in lecture form the material to be mastered. Now that books and other printed materials are more plentiful, the lecture persists as a method of teaching. Most often it is used by the teacher as a means of summarizing for the student that material which has been written in books.

In recent years the lecture has come in for some rather serious criticism. The way this method has been used, both in secular education and in religious education, probably justifies most of the criticism that has been raised against it.

When the lecture method is used with Juniors or Intermediates (surely no one tries to use it with younger children) disciplinary problems often arise. The class becomes inattentive and restless. The teacher can't understand why the children won't "sit still and listen." The lecture method is most often used in adult classes. It is true the teacher may not have observable disciplinary problems with this group. Adults have learned to sit still—but they do not always listen.

It is quite likely that many adults would say they like for the teacher to lecture. Undoubtedly one of the major reasons is that when this method is used class members have to make no response. They are not bothered or embarrassed by having questions asked. They can just sit quietly and listen. This is what they have been trained to do, and they enjoy the quiet comfort of a class session when the teacher is lecturing. Such teaching calls for no effort on their part either before, during, or after the class session. However, would the class members *learn* more if they did expend some effort, if they did participate in a lively discussion, if they did engage in some meaningful activity? The teacher must remember that his primary task is to help his members learn, not to entertain them. The lecture is effective only if, when the teacher acts, the members react either mentally, physically, or emotionally.

It is probable that the lecture method is the one that is most widely used in Sunday school teaching, particularly with older groups. This is rather strange in the light of the fact that the lecture is perhaps the most difficult of all methods to use *effectively*. Some teachers use the lecture because they think it is the easiest one to use. But this method is probably the most difficult of all to use to insure that learning will take place. This is not to say it is difficult to lecture. With sufficient material any one can go before a class and talk continuously for twenty to thirty minutes. However, while the teacher is talking he cannot be at all sure that he is teaching or that his members are learning. In too many Sunday school classes there has been a great deal of listening but altogether too little learning. It takes diligent research, careful organization of material, and forceful and dramatic presentation to make the lecture effective. In fact it is the unusual person who can use the lecture method so that it will be interesting and informing and so that results will be obtained.

Values

What has been said thus far might give the impression that the lecture method has no value. This, of course, is not true. It is a legitimate and useful way of teaching. It is not an easy method to use effectively, but it has its place along with other methods of teaching. In fact, the lecture has certain advantages over other ways of teaching.

Information.—Through a lecture the teacher may give information to the class that would be difficult if not impossible for the class to get. The teacher will have available teachers' helps, commentaries, and other materials which the class will not have. A discussion would be of absolutely no value here because the class does not have this information. The quickest and easiest way for the class to get this information is for the teacher to give it to them in the form of a lecture. This information may be of value for itself or for background.

Control.—When the teacher uses this method he has complete control of the teaching situation. He determines what material is to be used, what emphasis is to be given, and how much time is to be given to each point. In any lesson there is far more material given than can be used. In a given lesson one teacher may want to place the emphasis at one point, while another may place the emphasis at a different point. This is easiest to do when the lecture method is used.

Further, when the teacher uses the lecture method, he is better able to keep the lesson on the track. When the discussion method is used, the class may waste time on nonessentials. Or someone may lead the class down a blind alley. This can be avoided when the teacher lectures.

Time.—The lecture also saves time. This is a value of no little importance. The time for teaching the lesson is at best altogether too brief. There is so much about the Bible and the Christian way of life that class members need to know, to understand, to believe, and to practice. Valuable time may be consumed if the teacher pauses to ask or answer questions or to have the class to discuss a certain problem. Far more material may be covered in a given amount of time by using the lecture method. The danger here, however, is that the teacher may view teaching as "covering a certain material given in the lesson" rather than as causing learning and growth to take place. Covering a large body of material may be a hindrance rather than an aid to learning. Nevertheless, there are times when, for the sake of saving time, the best way to present given material is through a lecture.

Personality.—Another value is that the teacher may project the full power of his personality into the lecture. A dynamic lecture may have a ring of authority like that of the prophets with a "thus saith the Lord." This is one of the powers that the preacher has in the proclamation of the gospel. Having control of the organization of the material so that it points toward a climax and putting his own deepest feelings into the presentation of the lecture, the teacher is often able to stir the emotions of his class and inspire them to action in terms of higher Christian living. However, the teacher needs to be on guard lest the emotions which are thus stirred die in the classroom and fail to carry over into action outside the classroom.

Combination.—Finally, the lecture is a valuable method to use along with other methods in a given class session. The discussion thus far has been treating the lecture as though it would consume the entire class period. Actually a lecture may be any presentation in which the teacher does all the talking. It may take the entire session or it may be only a two- or three-minute statement by the teacher. The lecture method is most effective when it is used along with some other methods. Hardly a lesson will be taught in which the teacher does not do some lecturing. He may make a brief introduction; he may clear up some mistaken idea; he may introduce some new material. But along with this he will also ask and answer questions; he may have a brief discussion of a problem; he will tell a story or use an illustration. This use of the lecture along with other methods makes for greater interest, more participation, and better learning. It should be a relatively rare thing for the teacher to use the lecture method for the entire class session.

Limitations

As with all methods there are certain limitations or disadvantages to the lecture method.[1]

---

[1] Cf. C. B. Eavey, *Principles of Teaching for Christian Teachers* (Grand Rapids: Zondervan Publishing House, 1950), pp. 277–79.

Minimum participation.—Using the lecture method, the teacher has a minimum of the participation and activity which are so essential to learning. The class member may be listening but not learning.

Individual differences.—The lecture makes no provision for individual differences. The same material is given for the whole class. It may be that some in the class have excellent background in the area being taught, and the lecture may be only repeating what they already know. On the other hand, some may have no background in this area and do not understand what the teacher is talking about. Or, some in the class may have needs in this area that the lecture doesn't touch.

Attention.—When the teacher is lecturing, he does not know what the members are thinking. He does not know whether they are following the ideas presented in the lecture or not.

Questions.—Another limitation of the lecture is that the teacher does not know what questions may be in the minds of his members. Of course in the preparation of the lecture he will try to forecast the questions they might ask and undertake to answer them in the lecture, but at best this can be done only partially. If the lecture really stimulates the class, many questions will arise which the members would like to have answered. The practice of asking, "Are there any questions?" at the end of the class period will not make up for this limitation. The member wants to ask the question when it first comes to his mind and when the teacher is discussing the problem. If he has to wait until the end of the class, the subject has changed, the atmosphere is changed, and the question is not likely to be asked.

Contributions.—When the teacher lectures for the whole class period, he and the class miss the contributions by way of ideas and insights that the various members might have. No one person has all of the ideas, not even the teacher who has studied the lesson helps. It may be true that the class members do not have a knowledge of the Bible and the Christian faith they ought to have, but the depth of the insight some of the members

108

show when they are given an opportunity to express themselves is often surprising. This is what we mean when we say that teaching is the sharing of ideas and experiences leading to the growth of ideas and the enrichment of experience.

Skill.—A very practical limitation of the lecture method is that it requires skill in speaking and presentation that many teachers do not possess. It takes an artist who has a mastery of the field in which he is lecturing and who has a keen sense of the dramatic to be able to lecture effectively. Otherwise a lecture can be a drab, monotonous experience.

Frequent Use

If it is true that the lecture is one of the most difficult methods to use effectively, why is it used so extensively by teachers?

Wrong ideas.—Some teachers use this method because they have the wrong idea of what teaching is. They think that telling is teaching; they feel that they have taught when they tell their class what they have studied in the teacher's quarterly and other lesson helps during the week.

Time-saving.—Closely related to the above is another reason often given by teachers. They use the lecture because it saves time. To have questions and answers and discussions takes valuable time that the teacher could be using to give the class more information. Since there is so much the class needs to know and since there is so much material that ought to be covered in the brief time the teacher has for teaching, the lecture is the best way to cover the most material in the least amount of time. This, of course, is true. But involved here is another erroneous concept as to what teaching is—the concept that teaching is "covering a certain amount of material."

Habit.—Other teachers lecture from habit. This is the way they were taught, and this is the way they have always taught.

Ignorance.—Some teachers use the lecture because they do not know how to use any other method. They are reluctant to use a new way of teaching—such as question and answer, discussion, or role-playing—because they are afraid of failing. Therefore, even though they may realize that lecturing is not the most effective way to teach, they continue to use it because this is the method with which they feel most secure.

Lack of response.—Others use the lecture because they say they can't persuade their members to talk. This is one of the reasons most frequently given by teachers for using this method. It is likely that the teacher tried asking questions at one time, and when the members did not respond, he gave up trying. In spite of the fact that large numbers of teachers say they cannot get their members to talk, the experience of countless other teachers in many and varied situations proves that people do talk and that the members of a Sunday school class will respond when the lesson is properly approached by the teacher.

Control.—Probably the majority of teachers use the lecture method because the teacher always has the class under control. That is, he has all of his material prepared in advance, and he knows exactly what he is going to say. The class will not be disturbed by some knotty problem which will be difficult to solve. The teacher will not be embarrassed because some member asks him a question which he cannot answer. Thus, using the lecture, makes the teacher feel much more secure. He knows exactly what he is going to say next—it is in his outline.

Preparing the Lecture

The teacher is getting ready to prepare the lesson for Sunday. He has given some study to the lesson and feels that the lecture method would be the most effective approach to use. How does he go about preparing the lecture? Of course, there is no set pattern. The teacher must be free to express his own individuality. Following are some general suggestions the teacher might want to keep in mind.

Knowledge.—First, the one who would lecture should have an adequate knowledge in the area in which he lectures. This means that the teacher must give serious study to the Bible passage under consideration. This would include a study not only of the teacher's quarterly but also of Bible commentaries and other aids which may be needed by the teacher. The teacher ought to have far more information at his command than he will need for the lecture. If the lecture is to be stimulating, the teacher should lecture out of the overflow of his knowledge. No teacher should undertake to lecture on a "hand to mouth" basis.

Purpose.—Second, the teacher should determine clearly his purpose. What is it he wants to accomplish through his lecture? Does he desire to give new information and teach knowledge to the class? Or does he desire to inspire the class? He must know this because the approach he makes would be different in each case. If he desired to teach knowledge he would need to arrange the lecture so that this new knowledge could be grasped and retained. This is not done sufficiently in teaching and may be one reason people have such an inadequate grasp of Bible knowledge. On the other hand, if he desired inspiration he would need to arrange the lecture so that it would build to a climax in the conclusion.

Outline.—There are many different ways to outline a lecture. This is a simple plan: Introduction, Development, and Conclusion.

(1) *Introduction.*—At the beginning of the lecture the teacher must show the class why the material to be presented is important and how it is related to the lives of the members. He must give them a reason for listening. He must compel attention by making his lecture so captivating the members will want to listen. If the teacher does not capture his members in the introduction, they will not go with him through the rest of the lecture.

(2) *Development.*—How the teacher develops the lecture will depend upon the purpose he has chosen. If he desires to teach knowledge, he will go from the known to the unknown, from the familiar to the unfamiliar. He will also be careful about the rate at which the new knowledge is given. It must not be

given so fast that it cannot be assimilated. It may be that he will want the members to take notes, for this is an important aid in learning.

In determining his purpose and in developing the lecture the teacher must also take into consideration the needs and interests of the class members. If the lecture is to be meaningful to them, they must see clearly the relationship between the lecture and their own lives and problems. This means that in developing the lecture the teacher should seek to forecast the problems the members might face in this area and indicate how this Christian principle relates to these problems. He should also anticipate as fully as possible the questions that will come to his members and seek to answer these questions in his lecture. In doing so, the teacher is thinking *with* his members, and they are thinking *with* him. Thus the lecture takes on the "problem-solving" approach. In this way learning is much more likely to take place.

The teacher should have an outline that is so clear the members will be able to follow it without difficulty as the teacher moves from point to point. It is helpful if the teacher puts his outline on the chalkboard as he lectures. Usually it is best for the teacher not to put his complete outline on the board at the beginning of the lesson. To put it up as the lecture progresses makes for more interest on the part of the members.

(3) *Conclusion.*—The entire lecture should be brought to a climax in the conclusion. Here the teacher should seek conviction, commitment, application, and action.

Presenting the Lecture

It is Sunday morning. The time has come for the teacher to present his lecture to the class. The same rules that govern good public speaking in any other area are applicable here.

1. The teacher must make the material he has studied his own. One of the main reasons for listless lectures in Sunday school is that the teacher merely parrots materials which he

has read in the lesson helps. It is legitimate for a teacher to get ideas from these helps, but he should certainly make them his own by clothing them in his own words and manner of expression.

2. The teacher ought also to feel deeply about the material he is presenting in the lecture. One of the advantages of the lecture method is that it gives the teacher the opportunity to project the whole of his personality into the lecture. If the matter which he is discussing is not of deepest importance to him, his presentation will be lacking in force.

3. He should be himself. Of course, he can learn from others, but he should not imitate others.

4. He should begin quietly and build toward a climax. Particularly is this true if his aim is inspiration. Usually the entire lecture should be given in a conversational manner.

5. The teacher must keep in continuous contact with his members. One way this may be done is for the teacher to look into the eyes of his members as he speaks. It is quite distracting for the teacher to be constantly looking out of the window or at the corner of the room. Indeed the eyes can be a most powerful asset for the teacher. When he feels his message deeply, the eyes of the lecturer may help him penetrate his message into the souls of his members. In addition, by keeping eye contact with his members, the teacher is able to note their reaction to his presentation. He must be able to sense how they feel and almost know what they are thinking. If he notes that they are becoming restless or that they are not responding to the lecture, he may need to pause and ask a question, write on the chalkboard, use the map, or make some other appropriate adaptation to again secure the interest of the class.

6. He should use the whole range of his voice in presentation. He should not lull the class to sleep by using a dull monotone. This refers to the inflection of the voice, not to the volume. The teacher must suit the volume of his voice to the size of the classroom. The speed with which the lecture is delivered is also im-

portant. It should not be either too fast or too slow. If the attention of the members seems to be waning, a sudden change of pace is often helpful in reviving their interest.

7. Needless gestures and offensive mannerisms should be avoided. However, an element of the dramatic always makes the lecture more interesting.

8. The use of visual aids, such as the chalkboard, are helpful in keeping attention and in securing learning.

9. The teacher should always take care to make his outline clear. This may be done by putting it on the chalkboard while he is lecturing.

10. The use of good illustrations enlivens a lecture and aids the members in understanding and learning.

Lecturing with Profit

The lecture is a valuable method of teaching and may be used at times with real profit. Following are some suggestions. It is not to be implied, however, that the lecture should be used all of the time even in these instances.

1. It may be used to introduce a quarter's lessons. Here the teacher would seek to give the class the necessary background, to arouse within them an interest in the study by giving them a purpose for it, and to give them the general direction the study is to take.

2. It may be used to summarize a series of lessons. However, if the teacher's purpose is to give the class a review over a series of lessons, it is likely that the question and answer method should be used along with some lecture.

3. The lecture is often used to present material that would be difficult for the members to secure.

4. The lecture can be used quite effectively when the members lack the proper background information to discuss intelligently the matter under consideration. This is particularly true when the teacher is presenting technical material such as may be found in doctrinal lessons. However, the teacher ought

not to underestimate the background of the members. Some of these adults have been coming to Sunday school for twenty and more years. If they do not have sufficient background to discuss the Bible intelligently, it may be that they have been lectured to too often.

5. It may be used when the teacher has a knowledge aim in mind. It should be understood, however, that this is not the only method nor necessarily the best one to use with a knowledge aim.

6. It may be used when the time element is important. There are occasions when lack of time makes it imperative that the teacher lecture. On the other hand the teacher should never use this as an excuse to lecture all the time. It is true that the lecture is the most economical way of presenting a mass of material to the class, but it is not necessarily true that members learn best when they have a mass of material presented to them.

Guidance in Lesson Preparation

The time has come for the teachers to prepare the lesson they are to teach next Sunday. The superintendent should seek to help the teachers apply what has been studied as they prepare the lesson. He will lead them to consider and answer the following questions.

1. Why is the teacher using the lecture rather than some other method of teaching? To give new information? To introduce a quarter's lessons? To summarize a series of lessons? To give new or technical information to the members?

2. Is the lecture method to be used for the entire lesson? Or will the lecture method be used for only a part of the lesson and other methods be used also?

3. Does the teacher secure attention at the beginning of the lesson? How?

4. Is the teacher's aim in this lesson to teach facts? If so, does he provide in the course of his lecture frequent repetition and review for the class?

115

5. Is the teacher's aim in this lesson to give inspiration? If so, does the lecture lead to a climax?

6. Is the lecture clearly outlined?

7. Is the outline consistent with the teacher's aim?

8. Does the teacher have any plan to use visual aids, such as chalkboard or maps?

9. What illustrations are planned?

10. What questions that the members might have does the lecture answer?

9. The Story or Illustration

LET ME ILLUSTRATE!" "Here is an example!" What teacher has not seen an awakening of interest on the part of the class members for what is to follow when statements such as these have been made? The story has been used as a means of teaching since earliest times. Primitive peoples passed on their history and traditions through the use of stories. Jesus used this method with great effectiveness.

With small children the story has long been an accepted method of teaching. Often with this group the entire lesson is built around a Bible story. However, with Juniors, Intermediates, Young People, and Adults the story will usually take the form of an illustration, an example, an incident, or an experience. An illustration may be thought of as a brief story told for a particular purpose. It is used to make some point more vivid or clear. Although the illustration cannot strictly be called a method, it is a sufficiently valuable tool in teaching to merit consideration. The terms "story" and "illustration" will be used interchangeably in this discussion.

Relationship to Learning

The purpose of any method of teaching is to help learning to take place. How, then, is the story related to learning? A few of the ways are indicated here.

Interest.—Learning is based upon interest. As is well known, the story is one of the most effective means of stimulating pupil interest.

Insight.—Learning involves leading the learner to gain insight. The teacher wants to lead his members to say (at least silently) "I see it!" or "I understand that, now!" or "I had never seen it that way before!" The illustration is a valuable aid in leading the learner to this new or deeper insight.

Familiarity.—One of the principles of teaching and learning is to go from the known to the unknown or from the familiar to the unfamiliar. The story or illustration does this by explaining the less familiar in terms of the more familiar or by explaining something abstract in terms of something concrete.

Problem solving.—Learning involves problem solving. The story may introduce the class to a problem in real life. It indicates the conflicts and tells how the problem was solved. The learner, then, in his own mind, is led to face how he would seek to solve the same or a similar problem in his own life.

Purposes or Uses

The story or illustration may serve numerous purposes. In fact, it may serve several purposes at the same time. What are some of the purposes for which the story may be used?

Explanation.—It may be used to throw light on or explain a problem that is not clear or that is difficult to understand. Someone has suggested that when a teacher uses an illustration it is as though he were pulling back the curtain to let the light shine in.

Example.—An illustration may be used to give an example of the spiritual truth being taught. In so doing the teacher clothes the truth in flesh and blood. He shows what someone actually did under a given set of circumstances. This tends to take teaching out of the realm of the theoretical and brings it into the realm of life.

Persuasion.—Illustrations are often used to stimulate the hearers to action. Their purpose is to persuade as well as to instruct. Illustrations touch the feelings and elicit an emotional response. The idea behind the illustration is, usually, that this emotional response will lead the members to want to follow the example given in the story. "If he did it, I can too!"

Emphasis.—It is a valuable aid in helping the learners remember the truth being emphasized. It is a well known fact among all who preach, teach, or speak that the listeners often remember the stories or illustrations far longer than any other part of the presentation.

Attention.—A story or illustration may be used to secure attention or to deepen interest. Many public speakers, when they notice that their audience is becoming restless or inattentive, use an illustration to regain interest. However, two things need to be said in this connection. First, whenever the teacher uses a story to secure attention or deepen interest, it ought always to serve some other purpose also. That is, it ought also explain or give an example of the truth being discussed or stimulate to action. The teacher ought not simply tell a story, humorous or otherwise, which is wholly unrelated to the lesson merely to get attention or interest.

Second, because an illustration does deepen interest, the teacher is encouraged to use one or more in every lesson. Of course the teacher must guard against the over-use of illustrations. The lesson ought to be more than a series of illustrations which are held together by a flimsy thread of pious comments. On the other hand, illustrations do serve a most useful purpose, and the teacher is encouraged to make his lessons become vivid, alive, and meaningful by the wise selection and skillful use of good illustrations.

Sources

The reaction of the teacher undoubtedly is, "All this is fine, but where am I going to find good illustrations?" Actually, good illustrations may be found in many places. It is only necessary for him to look for them and have his eyes open so he can recognize them when he sees them. In other words, the teacher must become "illustration conscious," for when he does he will, as Shapespeare says, find "sermons in stones." For the teacher who has eyes to see there is a wealth of illustrative material all about him, even in the most commonplace happenings.

Jesus' sources.—Note from the ministry of Jesus how he used the most commonplace happenings and situations to illustrate deep spiritual truths.

(1) *Farm life.*—On one occasion he said that a sower went forth to sow. Some seeds fell on one type of ground and other seeds fell on other types of ground. Or, here was a man who had a bountiful crop. He tore down his old barns and built new ones and then said, "Soul, take thine ease."

(2) *Home life.*—A woman who lost a coin swept the whole house until she found it. A woman put leaven in bread and it leavened the whole. A certain man had two sons. One of them wanted his inheritance so he could go see the world. There was a wedding. Ten virgins were going to meet the bridegroom. Five had enough oil, five didn't.

(3) *Business life.*—A certain householder planted a vineyard. He let it out to certain husbandmen. These badly mistreated the servants the householder sent to collect what was due him. They finally killed his son. A man employed certain ones to work in his field for a certain salary. Shortly before quitting time he employed some others. At the end of the day he paid them all the same wage.

(4) *Political life.*—Jesus used a coin to answer the question about paying taxes, and in so doing he taught an even deeper truth. He said that one king who planned to do battle against another king ought to take counsel whether he could contend against the other king who had a superior force.

Personal experience.—One valuable source of illustrations is the teacher's own personal experience. The members usually are vitally interested in the experiences the teacher has had in the Christian life. This is personal religion; it is not something secondhand from the quarterly or some other source. Yet, valuable as this is, the teacher must guard against the overuse of personal experiences. Using them too often may become boring to the class.

Current events.—Current events is another source from which the teacher may glean stories, examples, and experiences. Jesus made use of current events. He spoke of those who had been killed by Pilate and whose blood had been mingled with their sacrifices and those upon whom the tower in Siloam had fallen to point out that all are guilty before God and thus must repent. As the teacher reads the newspapers and magazines, he may find numerous events and experiences that will illustrate the ideas he seeks to present to his class. Even the comic strips may be a source of help!

Nature.—The realm of nature has long been used as a source for illustrations. Jesus made frequent use of nature for this purpose. He spoke of the ravens of the air and the lilies of the field. He spoke of God's care of the sparrow. He told of a man's building his house on the sands; when the rains came and the wind blew, the house fell. The orderliness of the universe may be used to point to the orderliness and design of God. The quickening of life in the spring may be used to throw some light on the resurrection.

Biography.—Biography can be a real source of help to the teacher. The poet has said,

> Lives of great men all remind us
> We can make our lives sublime.

The experiences and achievements of others challenge; even their mistakes and failures encourage. There are the great men of history. There are the giants of Christian history. There are numerous illustrations that may be gleaned from the people of the Bible. There are the lives of the great missionaries, past and present.

Work.—There will be illustrations which the teacher will find in his own area of work. The lawyer will find many analogies and illustrations from law. The scientist or student of science will find excellent illustrations from this area. If the teacher is not a scientist and uses an illustration from this area, let him make sure that his facts are correct and that his application is accurate. Otherwise those who hear him teach may discredit both his illustration and the truth he is seeking to teach. The housewife will find many examples or illustrations from home life, the farmer from the farm, the mechanic from machinery, and the businessman from business.

Sermons.—Sermons and other types of speeches will be a source of help for the teacher. Good speakers almost always use good illustrations. The teacher ought to cultivate the habit of carrying small index cards with him and writing down good illustrations when he hears them.

Teachers' helps.—One of the most immediate sources of help for the teacher is the teacher's quarterly. The editors of the various lesson courses encourage the lesson writers to include suitable illustrations in every lesson. This does not mean that the teacher will be able to use every illustration given in the quarterly, but at least he can evaluate them to see whether they will be relevant to the lesson he is to teach.

Other teachers.—The teachers may share stories, examples, or illustrations with one another. This can be done easily and naturally during the teaching improvement period of the weekly officers and teachers' meeting. As the teachers sit around a table sharing their ideas while planning the lesson together, they may also share with each other the illustrations they plan to use. Again, this does not mean that every teacher will be able to use every illustration the other teachers plan to use. But sometimes he will get just the illustration he wants from a fellow teacher.

Perhaps a brief word should be said here about keeping or filing illustrations. If the teacher wants to make his lesson sparkle and come alive through the use of good illustrations, it will be necessary for him to keep a file. Whenever he reads, hears, or thinks of a good illustration, he ought to write it on a suitable card. These cards then will be filed under appropriate headings ready for use when needed. Of course this will involve some work for the teacher. Nevertheless, if he files the illustrations, he has them; if he doesn't, he forgets them.

Using Illustrations in a Lesson Plan

When and how may illustrations be used in a lesson plan? Actually they may be used at any point during the lesson.

Introduction.—A story or illustration may be used to introduce the lesson. This is an excellent way to begin a lesson, and the story then serves a two-fold purpose: it immediately secures the attention of the class, and it focuses attention on the central problem to be considered in the lesson.

Development.—It may be used in the development or "body" of the lesson. Usually the purpose of the illustration in this portion of the lesson is to clarify or deepen understanding. It may throw light on some difficult point being considered or it may give an example of the ideal being discussed.

Making the lesson personal.—It may be used in making the lesson personal. In this portion of the lesson the teacher seeks to lead the class members to see how the general spiritual truth being considered relates to their personal, everyday lives. He may use an illustration which shows how this truth affected one person's life.

Conclusion.—Finally it may be used in the conclusion of the lesson. When used here the illustration would serve as a climax to illustrate the desired application of the lesson.

Telling the Story

Two teachers may tell the same story, yet one of them may be far more effective than the other. The difference will be in the telling of the story. Following are some suggestions the teacher ought to consider.

Know the story well.—The teacher will certainly want to be well acquainted with all the details of the story and have all the events in proper order in his mind. Only in this way will he be able to tell it with confidence and without distracting hesitations.

See it clearly.—If possible the teacher should know the background out of which the story came. It will be to the teacher's advantage if he knows something of the social, political, and spiritual situation that surrounds a story from the Old Testament, for example. Such background knowledge will help him give color to the story. He will also be less likely to make incorrect statements. Equally important, the teacher ought to visualize the incident, happening, or story in his mind's eye until he sees every action and detail clearly. The members will not see the incident any more clearly or vividly than the teacher sees it and describes it.

Feel it deeply.—This is one of the biggest aids in telling a story effectively. As the teacher sees clearly the details of the incident, he must "feel" himself into the situation. Then he must tell it as he sees it and feels it. He needs to include descriptive and meaningful details. Here the teacher has an opportunity to use his creative imagination. The members will not feel the story any more deeply than the teacher feels it—and describes it.

Dramatize it.—The teacher needs to tell the story with some element of the dramatic. Of course moderation must be observed, but it is the task of the teacher to make the situation come alive for the class. Therefore the teacher ought not to be afraid of expressing his feelings as he tells the story. This is not merely a dry, mechanical recitation of facts. This is a life! Decisions hang in the balance! Therefore the words of the teacher ought to follow the action of the story. When the action is fast and intense, his words almost rush out. At other times his words will be slow and deliberate. At tense moments, a brief pause may be effective. Usually dialogue is better than direct discourse.

Build up to the climax.—This is the point of the whole story. This is the reason for telling it. In doing this all the elements of conflict must be realistically brought to the attention of the class. The decision to be made by the person in the story is not an easy one to make. Difficulties are involved; problems are encountered; his natural desires and human passions pull in the wrong direction! What will his decision be? This is the climax! The class must become emotionally involved in the situation.

End it quickly.—The good story ends quickly. Some may end with the climax. Others may need a sentence or two to round out the story. The teacher should not ramble here. He can ruin the effectiveness of the whole story.

Every teacher can become more adept at telling stories through practice. He needs to listen to others who are effective. He might not try to imitate them but seek to determine what makes their presentation effective and then use the same principles. The teacher should practice telling stories to himself when he is alone and then tell them to his class. Practice helps.

Qualities of a Good Story

What are the qualities of a good story?

Relevant.—First, the story ought to be relevant to the lesson and to the particular point being discussed. In other words, it ought to illustrate the point it is supposed to illustrate. Second, the illustration ought to be relevant to the life experience of the members. It may be a good illustration, but if it has no meaning for the life of the members, of what value is it? For example, a teacher is teaching a class of Junior boys a lesson on temptation. An illustration about a robber who stole ten thousand dollars from a bank would be less relevant than a story about a boy who was tempted not to pay his bus fare when the driver didn't see him.

Interesting.—A story that lacks this quality is not worth telling.

Accurate.—If the story is told for a true story, be sure it is true. It is permissible for the teacher to tell "made up" stories if the class understands clearly that they are "made up." The teacher may say, "Let us suppose such and such a situation—." The details of the story ought to be accurate. If the story is from the Bible, from history, or from biography the teacher ought to make sure of his facts.

Brief.—Because of limited time most stories the teacher uses ought to be brief. The stories of Jesus are all unusually brief.

Clear.—The characters involved, the problem confronted, the elements of conflict involved—all these things ought to be clear to the listener. It is frustrating as well as confusing for the listener to get so involved in a complex story that he gets the characters mixed up.

Fresh.—Well worn, overused stories or illustrations may distract from the lesson rather than add to it. It is usually better to omit the illustration altogether than to use one that is stale. Better yet, find one that is fresh and use it.

Guidance in Lesson Preparation

The superintendent will now lead the teachers in their preparation of the lesson for next Sunday. The following suggestions will help the superintendent as he seeks to help the teachers apply the method they have just studied.

1. The superintendent will lead the teachers to share with one another the illustrations they plan to use.

2. One teacher might demonstrate how he would tell one of his stories. The other teachers might analyze the points of strength and weakness in the manner of presentation.

3. After he has completed the preparation of the lesson, each teacher might go back over his lesson plan and check how many illustrations he has planned to use. Are there too many? Are there too few? There is no set rule as to number. It would vary from lesson to lesson.

4. The teacher might note the purpose of each of his illustrations.

(1) Does it serve to give an example of a truth?

(2) Does it serve to explain a truth?

(3) Does it serve to stimulate to action?

5. How does the illustration fit into the teacher's lesson plan?

(1) Is he using it in the introduction?

(2) Is he using it in the development of the lesson?

(3) Is he using it in making the lesson personal?

(4) Is he using it in the conclusion?

(5) Is he using an illustration in several of these areas?

6. Each teacher should evaluate his illustrations according to the following:

(1) Does it effectively illustrate the point?

(2) Does it sparkle with interest?

(3) Is it relevant to the experience of the group?

(4) Does it have emotional appeal?

(5) Are the facts accurate so far as the teacher can find out?

10. Role Playing

ROLE PLAYING is a relatively new educational technique. Because of their unfamiliarity with this technique many Sunday school teachers will be tempted either to ignore it or refuse to try it. This is to be expected, because teachers often are reluctant to leave established ways of teaching, in which they feel secure, to try something new. However, the department superintendent should lead his teachers to overcome this reluctance. Role playing can be a most effective way of teaching.

Definition

Children are often observed "playing Sunday school" or "playing house." In these games they reveal their feelings and attitudes. Sometimes mother and father have been embarrassed as they have seen themselves "scolding the children." Role playing is an adaptation of this "make believe play," in which the class may observe various attitudes expressed and evaluate the consequences of those attitudes. It is a brief, spontaneous, unrehearsed presentation of a problem in which certain members of the class act out certain roles. There is no script prepared, no memorizing of parts. It probably can be used best with Juniors through Adults. The problems which are enacted may deal with human relations or social situations (sometimes called sociodrama). Or the problems may deal with personal-emotional feelings (sometimes called psycho-drama). The inexperienced teacher will want to be careful about dealing with the personal-emotional feelings of the members, and it is likely that almost

all of the situations that will be enacted in the Sunday school
will deal with human or social relations.

An Example

Since this is a relatively new method of teaching, perhaps it
would be helpful to give an example in some detail before discussing the various aspects of the method.

Let us say the teacher is teaching a class of sixteen-year-old
boys. The lesson topic is "How to Live with Parents." The
Scripture passage is Colossians 3:18–25, including the verses,
"Children, obey your parents in all things: for this is well pleas-
ing unto the Lord. Fathers, provoke not your children to anger,
lest they be discouraged." The teacher's aim for the lesson is "To
lead my class to discover and to begin doing at least one thing
which will make their home a happier place in which to live."

Assuming that the class period is thirty minutes in length, the
teacher will have spent at least the first fifteen minutes leading
the class in a consideration of the Scripture passage. He will
have undertaken to lead them to understand the spiritual principles involved as these relate both to parents and to children.

Presenting the problem.—The teacher might then say, "Although we know and accept the ideal that as Christians we
ought to obey our parents, we often come into conflict with our
parents. In some homes these conflicts come quite often and
sometimes become rather heated. They always make us and our
parents unhappy. As Christians we ought to discover, if we can,
some ways to avoid at least some of these conflicts. If we could
it would certainly make our homes happier places in which to
live. I have a situation I would like for you to act out, and I
would like for you to be as serious about this matter as you can.
Some of the acting may be amusing to you but let no one laugh."

Selecting and instructing the characters.—The teacher asks
John to play the father and Sam to play the role of the son. He
gives these instructions to John (where the son and the others
cannot hear): "Your son is quite irresponsible. He doesn't pick

up his clothes; he doesn't help around the house. He thinks only of himself and what he wants to do. He's always wanting to go out. His selfish attitude often makes you mad. Now he is going to ask you to let him go out. You refuse. One word leads to another until the two of you are in a heated argument." These are the instructions to Sam (where the father and the others cannot hear): "Your father is always keeping you from doing what you want to do. He's always nagging at you. 'Don't do this; don't do that.' You come in and ask to go out tonight. He will refuse. You get mad. One word will lead to another until you are in a heated argument." The teacher will give the two actors a minute to "think themselves" into their roles while he instructs the class: "In this situation a typical father and son are talking. The son is going to ask to go out. Here are two questions I would like for you to keep in mind and discuss when the scene is over: What was the reason (or reasons) this conversation ended as it did? Could anything have been done to change it?"

Enacting the scene.—The two boys come in (they have been outside the classroom thinking of their roles but not discussing them) and present the scene, saying what they want to say. A minute or two after they have gotten into a heated argument, the teacher stops the scene.

Discussing the scene.—The teacher might ask John, "As father, how did you feel toward your son?" After he has expressed himself, the teacher might say to Sam, "As son, how did you feel toward your father?" After he has expressed himself, the teacher would ask the class the two questions he gave to them earlier. "What was the reason (or reasons) this conversation ended as it did?" He would seek to lead the class to get beneath the obvious fact that both of them were angry. Why were they angry? After this has been discussed the second question could be asked. Their ideas here will be most beneficial.

Replaying the scene.—After this discussion the teacher may say, "Now I would like for us to re-play this scene using a different approach." The same boys or different ones may be used.

The teacher will tell the boy playing the father's role to refuse to let the son go out and then react as he thinks a normal father would to whatever the son says. The son is to ask the father for permission to go out. When father refuses, he is to say, "Dad, I notice we have a lot of conflict over this problem. I also notice that there are a number of things I do that you don't like. Would you make a list of these and I'll work on them." The two boys then re-play the scene spontaneously.

Discussing the scene.—The teacher then could ask the class, "Would this approach to the problem make for a happier relationship between father and son?" After discussion the teacher may ask, "How does this relate to the spiritual ideal we were discussing in the first part of our lesson?" Help the class to see that the spiritual ideal actually *works* in helping people to have happier relations.

Setting a learning goal.—In seeking to have the lesson carry over into the lives of the members the teacher might say, "Can each of you think of one thing you might do this next week that will make relationships with your parents happier? Here are pencils and paper. When you think of something, you can write it down, and it can become for you a 'learning goal' that you will try to reach. Next Sunday we will discuss what you did and how it worked out."

Role Playing in the Total Lesson Plan

Role playing will not take the whole class period. Below is a possible lesson plan using role playing.

Introducing the lesson.—The teacher would begin the lesson, seeking to secure the interest of the class and to lead them in a serious reading of the Scripture passage.

Developing the lesson.—He would then lead the class in a more detailed consideration of the passage, helping them to come to understand more clearly the spiritual ideal involved. He would also seek to lead the class to accept this ideal as the way they ought to live.

Making the lesson personal.—It is at the point where the teacher seeks to relate the ideal to the personal lives of the members that role playing might be used. As the class is led to face some of the problems which confront them in their attempt at Christian living, a role-playing situation might help them see the problem more clearly and discover possible solutions in the light of the spiritual ideal.

Securing carry-over.—Carry-over into life might be secured as the teacher leads each member of the class, without putting any pressure on any of them, to set for themselves "learning goals" they will work on during the following week.

It is not suggested, of course, that role playing be used every Sunday. Like other methods, it should be used only when it would be the most effective method of helping the class learn a spiritual truth. In fact, this method probably should be used sparingly so that it does not become commonplace to the class and therefore lose its effectiveness. It should not be used by a teacher simply for the sake of using a "different" method.

Steps in Using Role Playing

What is the function of the teacher when this method is used? What are his responsibilities and how should he seek to carry them out? What are the steps that should be kept in mind?

Guide and direct.—First of all the teacher should view himself as the guide of the total process. Although in using role playing the class members are brought intimately into the teaching-learning situation, the teacher does not abdicate his position as teacher. It is his responsibility to guide, though not to dominate, the activity in such a way that maximum learning will take place.

Devise the problem to be acted out.—It is the teacher's responsibility to devise the situation the class is to portray. This will be done by the teacher during the time of lesson preparation. He certainly will not wait until he gets to class and depend upon some spur-of-the-moment impulse to give him the situation to be acted out. He should decide what problem is to be involved, what roles are to be portrayed, what instructions are to be given to each of the actors, and what questions the class is to discuss after the presentation. He might even decide tentatively what class members will play what roles. The importance of this advance preparation cannot be overemphasized.

In choosing a problem there are some things the teacher ought to take into consideration. (1) If this is the first time the class (or the teacher) has used this method, the problem to be presented should be simple and specific. (2) The problem must be meaningful to the class members. It must be real to them in terms of their own life experience. (3) The time element must be considered. The teacher must keep in mind how much time will be needed for other parts of the lesson and how much time will be needed for the presentation and discussion of the role-playing situation. Obviously this will be difficult at first, but with some experience, the teacher will be able to determine more accurately the amount of time needed.

Lead up to the problem.—How the role-playing situation fits into the total lesson plan and how the teacher is to lead up to the problem have been explained in a previous section.

Describe the problem.—After the teacher has led the class to see the relevance to their everyday lives of the spiritual ideal being studied, he then describes the problem to be acted out. He should present the problem so vividly that the group will become emotionally involved. Only then will they enter into the activity with seriousness of purpose.

Select characters.—The next step is for the teacher to select the individuals to portray the various roles. He must be careful to explain both to the class and to the actors that they are to act as they think the character they have been chosen to play would act—not as they, themselves, would act. If this is the first time this method has been used, the teacher should select those members he thinks can best carry out the roles. If there is an unfavorable role, the teacher will be sure to select someone who has enough self-confidence and enough status in the group that he will not be embarrassed. At first the class members will undoubtedly be shy and somewhat reluctant about taking part. For this reason the teacher should make sure that the situation to be acted out is one which is quite simple and one in which the class is deeply interested.

Instruct characters.—The teacher then instructs each of the characters. Usually this instruction should be given in private so the class does not know what specific roles are being portrayed. Also in most instances it is best for the teacher to instruct each individual actor in private so that the other actor or actors will not know what roles are being played. He should describe clearly to each the type of character he is to portray. He is not to tell them what they are supposed to say (except to get them started). He should encourage each one to respond spontaneously the way he thinks that character would respond. Then he will give the actors a minute or two to "think themselves into" the character they are to represent.

Instruct the class.—After he has instructed the characters, and while they are thinking over the part they are to play, the teacher will instruct the class. He gives them a general idea of the situation to be portrayed and tells them specifically what they are to look for. These questions will serve as the basis for discussion later on. Since some of the responses of the actors may be humorous, it will probably be well for the teacher to request the class to be serious and not to laugh during the portrayal.

Play the scene.—The actors are then called into the classroom and portray the scene. The teacher may need to remind one of the players of the role he is playing, but he should not do this unless it is absolutely necessary.

Stop the scene.—It is the responsibility of the teacher to stop the scene when it has gone on long enough. The temptation here is to let the action go on too long so that it begins to drag. The teacher will need to watch this.

Discussion of the scene.—This is one of the most important parts of the whole process. This is where the class is led to analyze and evaluate what they have observed. In this discussion they ought to come to deeper insights and to new discoveries of ways of acting as Christians. For this reason this part of the lesson ought to be carefully planned by the teacher.

Replay the scene if necessary.—On the basis of the discussion by the class, the new insights gained, and the suggestions made, it may sometimes be helpful to replay the scene, using characters who will make different responses as suggested by the class (or teacher). The same or different members may participate in this replay as the teacher may choose.

Setting goals for learning.—After the class has discussed the various possible responses and after they have identified what seems to them to be more Christian ways of responding, each member of the class should be encouraged (not pressured) to set for himself a "learning goal" toward which he will work. This is where the teaching done in the class session has the possibility of carrying over into the daily life of the class members.

Values and Limitations

As with all other methods, role playing has both values and limitations.

Values.—

(1) It is both an interesting and a stimulating technique for the teacher and the class members.

(2) It brings the class members actively into the teaching-learning process.

(3) It helps the members see and feel real problems in human relationships in a classroom setting.

(4) It provides an opportunity for the members to discuss more objectively certain situations that would be emotionally charged if they happened in real life.

(5) It leads the class to discuss attitudes which they would not normally express using the more traditional methods.

(6) By observing and acting out certain roles, the members are led to understand more clearly how other people feel and why they act as they do.

(7) It gives to the members an opportunity to experiment with new or different responses without suffering the consequences that might be experienced in real life.

Limitations.—

(1) Since this is a rather new technique, the teacher may be reluctant to use it because he does not know how it will turn out. Actually this is not a limitation of the method, but it ought to be considered. The superintendent should encourage his teachers not to be afraid to try out the new. Neither should they be afraid of failure. The first time this method is used, it may not work out perfectly. If it doesn't, the teacher will analyze why it didn't; he might list things that should have been done differently. The teachers should learn from their mistakes and keep on trying until they can use this method with success. The results in more effective learning will be worth the effort.

(2) Because it is new to the class members, they may be shy and hesitant about participating. For this reason the situation chosen to be portrayed should be quite simple. Great care should also be exercised by the teacher in selecting the members to participate.

(3) Some of the characters to be portrayed may be humorous, and the class may miss the seriousness of the problem being studied. This will more likely happen in the Junior and Intermediate groups. Those who teach these ages will need to be on guard against this situation.

(4) The class may engage in idle discussion and fail to identify the learnings that should come from the role-playing situation. The fault here is not with the method but with the teacher. Through careful planning and skilled leadership of the discussion, the teacher must make sure that the class identifies the problems involved and sees clearly the implications of the various responses that were made.

(5) This method cannot and should not be used all the time. It should be used only with those lessons that deal with problems in human relations. If it is overused, it will lose much of its effectiveness.

(6) Because role playing and the discussion which follows take much time, the teacher will not have as much time for Bible study as when other methods are used. On the other hand, the problems about which the Bible speaks will be made more vivid for the class when this method is used.

Guidance In Lesson Preparation

The department superintendent will guide the teachers in their preparation of the lesson they are to teach Sunday and seek to help them apply what they have been studying.

Perhaps it would be helpful if the superintendent would prepare in advance a situation that the teachers might role play briefly so they can get the "feel" of this approach. This situation would not necessarily have to be in line with the lesson to be taught Sunday.

These are some points the superintendent will want to lead the teachers to keep in mind as the lesson is being prepared.

1. Can role playing be used effectively in this lesson? There are many lessons with which it cannot be used. The superintendent should plan to use the study of this method when the teachers have a Sunday school lesson to which it can be applied.

2. The teachers will identify a central problem in the lesson about which they might devise a role-playing situation.

3. Then they will prepare the first part of the lesson. How will they seek to get the interest of the class in the introduction? How will they develop the lesson so that the class will understand and accept the spiritual ideal in the lesson?

4. The teachers will devise the problem.

5. Is the problem meaningful to the class?

6. How shall the teachers present the problem to the class so the members will feel it deeply?

7. What instructions are to be given to each of the participants? The teachers should write out these instructions in some detail.

8. What instructions are to be given to the class? What are they to look for? This also should be written out.

9. How shall the teacher lead the class in discussion after the scene is played?

10. Will the class need to replay the situation?

11. How will the teacher seek to lead the members to set "learning goals" for themselves as the result of this lesson?

11. The Project

WHAT IS A PROJECT? Some have viewed it as a specific technique. Others have said it was any activity the class members did together. Some have emphasized the planning aspect. They say the project is an activity in which the members participate in all stages of the activity. Still others have called it a principle, an attitude, a point of view rather than a specific method. These technical distinctions need not concern us. For our purpose we may say simply that a project is an activity in which the class engages either to deepen or to express the learning which they have done.

The project method is not new. It was used as a means of teaching and learning in primitive times when a father took his son on a hunting or fishing trip to let him learn by doing. It is used today in many normal life situations. The father supervises as the son makes his kite. The mother guides as the daughter bakes her first cake. Agricultural organizations for young people encourage their members to engage in projects such as planting a strawberry patch, caring for a calf, marketing a crop, piecing a quilt, or making a dress. The teacher takes this means of teaching and learning into the classroom and calls it a project.

Many Sunday school teachers of today have led their classes in projects without knowing they were using a project. They simply felt this or that activity was a good way to help the class to learn. Some have led classes to make blocks representing the books of the Bible and then to use these blocks in memorizing the books of the Bible. Others have led the class to help a family in need. This approach is simply a recognition by the teacher that all teaching is not done by telling and all learning is not done by listening. It is a recognition that there are certain Christian truths that are not really learned until they are expressed in life.

The Project and Learning

People may learn in many different ways. The closer learning is related to direct experience the more probable it is that the learning will be meaningful and lasting. The further the learning is removed from direct experience the more difficult it becomes.

Experience and common sense suggest that when the learner is merely *listening* to words someone says, he may be virtually inactive; he may respond but tentatively; he may be but little changed in his attitudes or even ideas for having listened. On a higher level of efficacy as a method of learning (because it involves the learner more fully himself) is *observation* on his part—seeing, either through pictures or going to see for himself. Yet even here the learner may remain merely spectator, giving but little of himself and gaining but little.

On a much higher level of effectiveness, because the learner is involved more deeply, is learning through *vicarious experience*. The learner moves over from the role of spectator to feeling—with a person or situation. On the highest level, because potentially involving the learner more fully, is firsthand, *direct experiencing*. [1]

One of the most effective ways to learn is to "learn by doing." A young lady learns to be a mother only by being a mother. A teacher may tell her something of the love and concern a mother has for a child, but she never really knows this love and concern until she comes into that relationship in which she is the mother of a child. This love and concern must be experienced;

---

[1] Clarice M. Bowman, *Ways Youth Learn* (New York: Harper and Brothers, 1952), p. 91. Used by permission.

it is born in a relationship. Then the many duties of motherhood are learned by experience. In something of the same way, one learns to be a Christian by being a Christian. One truly knows Christ only as he comes into a personal relationship with Christ. The life of the Christian is to be learned through experience, not through listening to some teacher talk about being Christian. This does not mean that one must engage in a project in order to be Christian. It simply means that Christianity should be expressed in experience, and this expression, may, at times, take the form of a project.

Too often Sunday school classes are places where big issues are discussed but little is done about them. On a given Sunday the class may discuss some major matter involved in the Christian faith. But they do not have time—or do not take time—to come to any positive conclusion. Only generalized applications are made, and the teacher exhorts the class to follow them. But no definite decisions are made, and no plans are laid to express the Christian truth that has been studied. The members leave, too often to do nothing. The next Sunday the lesson is on a different topic, and the class talks about this topic in the same way with still no decisions or plans for expression. And so it goes, Sunday after Sunday. In all this the members are learning, but what are they learning? They *may* be learning that all they do in Sunday school is come together and *talk*.

If this situation exists in the Sunday school class, it is a situation the teacher wants to change. He wants to lead his members to express their Christian faith. He wants to lead them to do something about the Christian ideals, truths, and attitudes that are discussed in the class. The project is one of the best means the teacher has for securing carry-over from the classroom to the lives of the members.

Types

What are the different types of projects in which a class might engage? The divisions suggested below are based on the

141

functions which the projects are to serve. Actually, there are no clear-cut distinctions as to type. A given project may serve more than one function and may be listed under more than one type. The following classification is given only to help the teacher see more clearly something of the variety of projects in which the class may engage.

Information.—The primary purpose of this type of project is to lead the members to secure and master certain information. A class of Juniors may be studying a series of lessons on "The Church." They may be led in a project in which they relate this study to their particular church. Various members might be requested to make a special study of the history, the financial program, the missionary activities, the service activities, and so forth, of their church. A class of Intermediates may be having a series of lessons on doctrines. In this study they find many theological words which they do not understand. They may decide to work together and make a brief theological dictionary for themselves. In doing this they would study the various theological terms and write out the meaning of each one in language they can understand. (Many Adult classes would profit from such a project.)

Attitude.—The primary purpose of this type of project is to change, to develop, or to deepen certain attitudes. The teacher might desire to help the class develop a deeper sensitivity toward those who are in need. He might take his class of Intermediates on a tour of the slum area on Saturday night. Or the class might be studying a lesson on temperance. One member might say that those who drink hurt only themselves. To see whether this is true the teacher may take the class to police headquarters and have an officer tell them about the relation of drinking to accidents. Or the teacher may take the class to visit an emergency room of a large hospital on a Saturday night.

Habits.—The primary purpose of this type of project is to develop certain desirable habits. The teacher of a class of Juniors may have noticed that the group is doing a number of things in the church which indicates a lack of reverence, such as talking in the worship assembly or the church service, writing notes, dropping song books on the floor, or running in the halls. He may seek to lead them in a project to be more reverent. Another teacher may find from the Training Union leader that the members of his class rarely read the Bible during the week. This teacher may lead the class in a project to develop the habit of daily Bible reading. Another teacher finds that the members of his class do not attend the preaching service regularly. The teacher may lead the class in a project to attend the worship services regularly. The teacher of an Adult class may lead his members to start having daily family worship. These and other desirable habits may be started by leading the class to engage in a project.

Service.—The primary purpose of this type of project is to give expression to a Christian ideal that is accepted, to meet some need that is recognized, or to render service in some area. This is the type of activity with which the teacher is probably most familiar. He has often led classes to help those in need. Juniors or Intermediates are led to visit those who are invalids and perhaps hold a religious service for them. These same groups go to jails, old people's homes, and the like to conduct religious services. Or the class may be led in a project of visiting the absentees.

One Intermediate group became deeply concerned about the displaced people of Hungary a few years ago. They decided to do something more than talk: they gathered clothes at home and from neighbors, secured boxes, packed the clothes, and sent several hundred pounds of much needed clothing to these people. One church was beginning a building program. The Juniors and Intermediates were challenged to do something worthy to contribute to the program. They decided on a work project. Everything they made from this work they would contribute to the building fund. The members of the church were encouraged to let them do odd jobs. They cut lawns, painted garages, did baby sitting, and washed cars. In six weeks' time they gave $2,000 to the building program. In so doing they came to have a greater appreciation and a deeper love for their church.

The class project may be quite simple to plan and quickly and easily carried out. To lead a class to write their congressman about some pending legislation would be a simple project. Or the project might be complex, requiring much more time in planning and executing. Class members might decide that they want to do something about providing a more wholesome environment in the community for the young people. This would necessitate study as to what the present situation is, what the young people are doing with their leisure time, and what needs to be done.

Projects may take place either in class or outside the class. If a Junior class is making a map of the Holy Land, they may spend a few minutes of the class period each Sunday working on it. But because of the pressure of time most of the projects of necessity will take place outside the class period. The project may be a group activity or an individual activity. If the class members decide to visit the city hospital, this would be done as a group. If they decide that they want to start daily family worship, they do this as individuals.

Steps in Guiding a Project

From the above discussion it will be seen that the project has two primary uses. First, it may be used to aid the class in learning, i.e., making a dictionary of theological words. Second, it may be used by the class as a means of expressing in a practical activity a spiritual ideal they hold, i.e., helping someone in need. It is obvious that the success of any project depends largely on proper preparation. While the planning of the actual project chosen will be done by the members in the class period, the preliminary consideration of possible projects that may be chosen and the consideration of what would be involved in the various projects should be made by the teacher at the time he prepares

144

his lesson. What then are the steps the teacher should keep in mind as he plans his lesson? These steps should be clearly understood by each teacher.

Need felt by the class.—If the class is to be led in a project, it should be based upon a need that is felt by the class. If the activity is to be meaningful to the group, they must feel that it is important. They must see clearly the reason for it, and they must *want* to do it. This felt need should grow out of the discussion of the Sunday school lesson. For this reason the teacher must plan his entire lesson with a possible project in mind. In the discussion of the lesson the teacher would hope that the class would develop both a sense of need and a desire to do something about that need.

Possible responses.—As the teacher prepares his lesson he should consider the various possible activities in which the class might engage in carrying out the lesson objective. From this group he probably will select one that seems to him to be best. However, in the class session the teacher should encourage the members to suggest possible projects. It may be that they will want to engage in an activity which the teacher has not selected. If their selection is worthy in light of the Christian gospel, and if it is attainable in terms of time and the ability of the class, their suggestion should be followed.

Project chosen.—It has just been stated that it is best for the class members to suggest and choose the project in which they wish to participate. This does not mean that the suggestion concerning a particular project will not come from the teacher. There will certainly be many times when this is the case. However, when the suggestion does come from the teacher, it should be quickly taken over by the class. The project is helpful to the class only when it is enthusiastically accepted. It should be engaged in because the members want to do it, not because the teacher wants them to do it. If the class does not so respond, it is better for the teacher to let the project drop. For a project to have spiritual benefit it must have a spiritual basis.

145

Plans made.—After the class has chosen a project, the members should be led to make the plans necessary for carrying it out. These plans should be made in the class session. Does the class need more information? Who is to get it? Are committees needed? How is the project to be carried out? When is the group to meet? Specific responsibilities should be accepted by various members. It is the task of the teacher to stimulate and guide, not to dominate in making these plans.

The teacher is cautioned to save ample time in the class session for the discussion of possible projects, for decisions, and for planning to carry out the project. The amount of time needed will depend on the nature and complexity of the project. The teacher should take this time factor into consideration and plan the other parts of the lesson so that sufficient time is left for this. If the bell rings or the class period comes to an end before all plans are complete, much of the value of the proposed activity will be lost.

Project carried out.—The activity chosen will usually be carried out outside the class session. However, certain activities may be engaged in for a few minutes during succeeding sessions, i.e., memorizing the books of the Bible, making a map of the Holy Land. As the project is carried out, it is the task of the teacher to supervise, guide, and encourage.

Evaluation of the project.—This step is not always necessary, but there are certain types of projects where an evaluation and discussion for learning values would be most beneficial. The class might consider such questions as: Was the project satisfactorily planned? What portions went well? What portions went poorly? What were some of our weaknesses? How can we do better next time? What values has the experience had for us?

Values

A method of teaching is used because it helps learning to take place. What are some of the values for learning of the project?

1. It makes learning more interesting.

2. The class learns through a meaningful, self-chosen activity.

3. A project often deepens the individual's sensitivity to and concern for the needs of others.

4. It develops leadership abilities as the class members assume and carry out various responsibilities.

5. It teaches co-operation as the members work together.

6. It deepens the awareness that religion is to be expressed, not merely talked about in church.

7. The members learn as they carry out the activity. For example, if the class decides to engage in a missionary project, helpful service will be rendered. In addition, while the members are engaged in this activity, they will probably learn more about a real missionary spirit than they would listening to a teacher in a number of class sessions.

8. It makes learning more lasting and more meaningful.

Cautions

There are certain cautions that ought to be given to the teachers as they contemplate using projects.

1. The teacher should make sure that the proposed activity is related to the learning which the teacher desires. The teacher must be careful not to lead the class in a project just so they will be engaged in some activity.

2. The teacher should be careful not to impose the activity on the class members. It must be freely chosen.

3. As the class engages in a project, particularly a service project, the teacher should take care that the members do not develop a pharisaical spirit or a holier-than-thou attitude. For example, if the class is seeking to help a group of underprivileged people they must not do it in a condescending attitude. They should feel with and identify themselves with the group they seek to serve.

4. Using a project takes time. It takes time for discussing and planning in the class session. It takes time, both of the teacher and the members, to carry it out. The teacher and the members

must be willing to give the time; the learning values and/or service rendered must be worth the time expended.

5. The teacher should avoid the overuse of projects. The lessons in which a project may be used should be selected by the teacher with great care. One cannot say just how often a project should be used. The responsiveness of the class is one factor to be considered. The type of lesson being taught is another factor. The difficulty of the projects planned is still another factor. Simple projects in which the younger age groups will more likely engage may be used more frequently. The more complex and difficult projects will be used less frequently.

Guidance in Lesson Preparation

The department superintendent should use this topic only when the teachers have the type of lesson with which a project may be used. The superintendent will lead the teachers in their preparation of the lesson, helping them determine what their aim will be, how they will begin with interest, and how they will seek to develop the lesson so the class will have both a sense of need and a desire to meet this need. It is at this point that they will consider how a project may be used.

The following questions are given for guidance.

1. What project (or possible projects) does the teacher have in mind in which the class might engage?

2. Is the project directly related to the lesson aim the teacher has in mind?

3. Is the total lesson as planned by the teacher sufficiently interesting and meaningful that it has a good possibility of stimulating the class to want to engage in a project?

4. How does the teacher plan to lead the class to face the question "What can we do about it?"

(1) Is the project to be initiated by the class? If so, how does the teacher plan to stimulate and encourage the class to initiate it?

(2) Does the teacher plan to initiate the project himself? If so, how does he plan to do so and still not dominate the class?

(3) Is the teacher ready to adapt himself if the class chooses a project that is different from the one he has planned?

5. What plans will the class need to make to carry out the project?

6. What plans are made to evaluate the project and discuss the learning values of the experience?

7. Have the steps in planning a project been noted and followed?

8. How much time will this part of the lesson take? Is the rest of the lesson planned so that sufficient time is left for this part?

12. Nonprojected Visual Aids

M R. JOHNSON, WHEN THE FOUR MEN let their friend down through the roof to Jesus, why didn't they fall off? How did they climb up on the roof with their sick friend?" Johnny, a ten-year-old Junior, was asking his teacher a question that had been bothering him throughout the lesson period. Of course Mr. Johnson could have explained that the roof was flat. But how much better it would have been for Johnny if his teacher had shown him a picture of a flat-roofed Palestinian house with steps on the outside wall from the ground to the roof. The teacher could have explained that the Jewish people often dried fruit in the sun on the roof, or sat there in the cool of the evening, or prayed there as Peter was doing when he saw a vision (Acts 10:9). A picture would have made the teaching far more vivid than the use of words alone.

Visual aids are being used increasingly for teaching and training in many areas. Children are familiar with the value of visual aids, both projected and nonprojected, through their use in the public schools. The armed services and businesses are using them extensively. There is ample experimental evidence that the use of visual aids helps a person learn more, learn faster, and remember longer. Surely Christian teachers will want to make use of these effective aids to enhance learning in the Sunday school.

Indeed, there are certain difficulties that inhere in teaching the Bible which make the use of visual aids almost imperative. The Bible is an ancient book, dealing with the life and customs of an ancient people. Something is needed to make these people and their customs come alive. When Jesus told the man to take up his bed and walk, what kind of bed did he have? Mary "brought forth her firstborn son, and wrapped him in swaddling clothes." What are "swaddling clothes"? A picture could make this clear for a class. The Scripture also says she "laid him in a manger." Was this unusual? What type of house did the average Jew live in? Did his animals live in the house with him? The use of visual aids would make these customs clear.

In this consideration of the use of visual aids in teaching nonprojected aids will be discussed first. This is done not by accident. When the average teacher thinks of visual aids, he often thinks only of the projected aids such as the motion picture, slides, and filmstrips. It is true that the projected aids have more "glamour," but in the Sunday school it is highly probable that the nonprojected aids will be used far more often. Nonprojected aids are inexpensive; they are already in many classrooms; they are simple to use. Teachers need to be led to use more effectively those visual aids that are already available. A partial list of nonprojected aids would include chalkboards, maps, flat pictures, field trips, bulletin boards, objects, models, charts, graphs, and drama. The first four of these will be considered in some detail. The others will be discussed only briefly.

Chalkboard

The term "chalkboard" is used in this discussion rather than the more traditional term "blackboard" because most of the boards being used today are light green rather than black.

It is probable that the chalkboard is the most versatile visual aid which the teacher has at his disposal. If all the visual aids, both projected and nonprojected, were to be evaulated in terms of ease of use, accessibility, effectiveness, and cost, it is quite likely that the chalkboard would come out on top. Yet the tragedy is that having this valuable teaching tool at hand teachers so often do not make use of it.

Advantages.—What are some of the advantages of the chalkboard?

(1) It is economical. It is relatively inexpensive to purchase and can be erased and re-used repeatedly.

(2) It is readily accessible. The teacher does not have to gather pictures in advance nor bring in equipment. It is there when he needs it.

(3) It is easy to use. All one needs in order to use the chalkboard is to know how to write.

(4) It focuses the attention of the class. It is almost automatic for a class to watch what is being written on the chalkboard. The teacher might try an experiment like this. While he is lecturing to the class, he might have someone write something on the chalkboard. The eyes of the class members will turn to watch what is being written on the board even though they know they are supposed to be listening to the teacher. The chalkboard is a great aid for the teacher of any age group. When attention seems to be lagging, the teacher can turn to the chalkboard and write something meaningful and related to what he is saying. The attention of the class will focus on what has been written.

(5) Perhaps most important of all, the chalkboard aids learning. The teacher has two opportunities to get his teaching across —when he presents it verbally and when he puts the key ideas on the chalkboard. It has been estimated that from 75 to 90 per cent of what is learned is learned through the eye. If this is true, how important it is for the teacher to appeal to the eye as well as the ear!

Types.—There are several different types of chalkboards from which to choose. For the department assembly a board on a stand with rollers is a good choice. In the classroom the teacher will need to decide between one that is permanently installed or one that is movable. The size will depend on available space. The teacher should guard against getting one that is too small. He may also choose a combination chalkboard and bulletin board. As to color, a good shade of green seems to be best. A movable board is recommended if it can be hung so that it will not wobble when the teacher writes on it. Purchasing a cheap board is false economy. Washing a chalkboard is the quickest way to ruin it. The chalkboard should be cleaned only with a clean eraser.

Use.—The use of the chalkboard is limited only by the ingenuity of the teacher. Here is a partial list of some possible uses. Teachers will be able to add to this list.

(1) To emphasize ideas given by the teacher.

(2) To list ideas or suggestions given by the class. To do this helps the group visualize their thoughts and be better able to evaluate them.

(3) To put contrasting or opposing positions before the class for consideration.

(4) To clarify new or unfamiliar words.

(5) To place statistics before the class. Statistics that are only spoken are quickly forgotten and often never really understood.

(6) To present the outline of the lesson.

(7) To make drawings or sketches.

(8) To draw maps.

(9) To draw graphs or charts.

(10) To present the records of the class or department.

Principles of utilization.—Following these simple principles will make the teacher's use of the chalkboard more effective.

(1) He should plan, as a part of his lesson preparation, how he will use the chalkboard. Will he outline the lesson? Will he list ideas presented by the class? Will he list contrasting ideas? Will he use a sketch, drawing, or graph? This does not mean that there will not be many times when the teacher will use the chalkboard on the spur of the moment. It simply means that some basic plans should be made in advance.

(2) All material placed on the chalkboard should be in line with the learning that is desired.

(3) Obviously the material on the chalkboard should be readable. First, the writing should be large enough for all in the class to see. Second, it should be written as clearly as possible. The teacher does not need a beautiful handwriting, but he should take some care when he writes on the chalkboard to see that his handwriting is legible.

(4) The material should be simple and as brief and concise as possible. Often a word or a phrase can carry the meaning of a whole sentence. At best, most classroom chalkboards are small. The teacher can make the most of the space by being concise.

(5) The teacher should be careful not to put too much material on the chalkboard at one time. As a general rule the teacher should *not* put the outline of the entire lesson on the chalkboard before or at the beginning of the class. Interest on the part of the class members is sustained more effectively if each point or division of the lesson is put on the board as the teacher comes to it. Interest is held better if the class does not know what is coming next. Also the act of writing on the board will serve to direct the attention of the class to the point being emphasized at the moment.

(6) The teacher will be careful to erase all unrelated material. Writing or markings other than that which the teacher is using tends to distract the class. It is best to start with a clean chalkboard each Sunday.

Maps

If the chalkboard is the most neglected visual aid in Sunday school classes, the map is the second most neglected aid. Too often teachers have maps in the classroom and never refer to them. Current world events have made people familiar with places they have never even heard about before. Thus the map can and should become for the Christian teacher an increasingly important teaching aid.

Types.—There are several different types of maps needed in the classroom. However, the cost involved in purchasing several maps for each class makes the problem of selection exceedingly difficult. Some churches purchase a number of maps and keep them in the church library to be checked out by the teachers as they are needed. Yet it is likely that on a given Sunday a number of teachers will need the same map, and there may not be enough to go around. It is suggested that the church contact the denomination or state visual aids workers for guidance in selecting maps for classroom use.

(1) The globe is the most accurate of all maps since it is the same shape as the earth. Yet it has two practical disadvantages. First, it is small and, when studying a country like Palestine, the details will be lacking. Second, it is often difficult to find a place to keep it in the classroom. It could be kept in the church library.

(2) A relief map shows the topography of the land, indicating the mountains, plateaus, and valleys. This type of map would help the class members understand the statement of Jesus that the good Samaritan "went down from Jerusalem to Jericho."

(3) A flat map is the type most commonly used in Sunday schools. Flat maps of Bible times are available in various designs:

a. *According to historic period.*—The teacher may secure a map of Palestine during the time of Abraham, Palestine during the period of the divided kingdom, or Palestine during the time of Jesus. A look at the maps in the back of your Bible will show the difference in them.

b. *According to purpose.*—There is a map showing the wandering of the Israelites in the wilderness, one showing the missionary journeys of Paul, another showing the events in the life of Jesus, and another showing modern mission fields.

c. *According to area.*—The teacher may secure a map showing only the land of Palestine, a map of Babylon and Palestine on which to trace the journey of Abraham, of Egypt and Palestine on which to trace the journey of the Children of Israel to the Land of Promise, or a map of the entire Near East on which to trace the journeys of Paul.

(4) If at all possible the teacher should own a Bible atlas. Certainly one or more copies should be in the church library for reference. The atlas contains maps, illustrations, and information about geographical locations and historical events.

Pupil-made maps.—The pupil-made map may be thought of as a type of map, but because of its value as a teaching aid it is lifted out for special consideration. The class may be led in a project to make a map showing the topography of Palestine. A simple paste made of flour, alum, and salt may be used. In order to make the map the members will have to make a careful study of the land of Palestine and its mountains, valleys, and rivers. In making such a study they will probably learn more about Palestine than they would in almost any other way. A flat map (or drawing) may be made of the journeys of Paul, the life of Jesus, or the journeys of Abraham, showing the events that happened in the various places. In making these maps the emphasis is not on the excellence of the map but on the information learned. The opportunities for teaching through this medium are numerous. Since this learning tends to be permanent, the teacher is encouraged to use it.

Purposes.—There are several purposes which a map may serve in teaching.

(1) To show the location of a city or country, i.e., Joppa, Nazareth, Judah, Samaria, Assyria.

(2) To show the type of country in which an event took place, i.e., the land of the wilderness wanderings.

(3) To trace a journey, i.e., the missionary journeys of Paul.

(4) To show relationships and distances, i.e., from Dan to Beersheba.

(5) To relate Bible events to modern geographical locations.

Principles of utilization.—Like any other teaching aid, the map must be used properly for maximum benefit. Here are some suggestions.

(1) The map must be available when it is needed.

(2) This means that the teacher must plan in advance when and how the map is to be used. This should be done as the teacher prepares his lesson. He will have the map in the class-room and will be sure it is the right type of map. He will know exactly how and for what purpose the map is to be used.

(3) The map must be large enough to be seen by all in the class. This is perhaps the most common failing in the use of maps. The teacher points to a place on the map but all the class sees is the finger of the teacher pointing to an unrecognizable blur. The class should be small enough to permit close observation of the map, or the map should be large enough for all to see.

(4) The teacher will make sure the class understands the scale and symbols used on the map. Let the class know whether one inch represents one mile, or ten miles, or fifty miles.

(5) Finally, the teacher will use the map at the opportune moment. When the question is asked or when the information is needed is the time to use the map.

Flat Pictures

Flat pictures have been used most extensively with small children. Often the denomination provides special teaching pictures which are correlated with the lesson for the Nursery, Beginner, Primary, and Junior departments. These are inexpensive and quite good. Those who teach these age groups will certainly want to make use of these pictures. However, flat pictures can be used effectively with all age groups. These may be found in books, newspapers, magazines, and other places.

Pictures have definite values in teaching. They can be used to help the class understand that which is unfamiliar, such as the dress, people, land, and customs of Bible times or of foreign countries. These pictures are easily available and are either free or inexpensive. The enterprising teacher will find numerous pictures for use. From the denomination's foreign and home mission journals, the *National Geographic*, or similar magazines the teacher will find many pictures that will be enlightening and meaningful to his class members regardless of their age. From newspapers and magazines also will come pictures which illustrate points of the lesson. The teacher needs to become picture conscious and clip pictures whenever they are found. Pictures used repeatedly should be mounted and filed.

There are many different ways to use pictures. They may be used to attract attention and stimulate interest in introducing a lesson. If the lesson is on the alcohol problem, a series of whiskey advertisements cut from magazines may be used. The teacher may find a picture of an automobile accident caused by a drunken driver. This will direct the attention of the class to the problem to be considered in the lesson. Or, pictures may be used to illustrate a point the teacher is making. A picture may show the hunger of people in certain areas or it may show a slum area. A picture may be used to give information, i.e., showing the dress or customs of people in Bible times.

When using flat pictures, certain principles should be observed by the teacher. The picture should be made an integral part of the total lesson plan. This means that the teacher must plan in advance when and how the picture is to be used. The picture itself should be large enough to be seen clearly by all in the class or some arrangement should be made for the class to view it at close range. The teacher should direct the members as they view the picture. He should tell the group what to look for so they will not miss the idea for which the teacher used the picture. Pictures should not be used too hurriedly; the members need time to study the picture.

Field trips

A field trip or observation trip gives the class a firsthand experience with something that cannot be brought into the classroom. It differs from a trip taken as a project because, in a project, service to be rendered is the primary motive. A field trip is a trip taken with an educational motive primarily in mind. It is a visual aid to learning. Almost always the trip will be taken at some time other than the regular class meeting time.

Steps to be followed.—For the class to derive maximum benefit from a field trip, there are certain steps which should be followed carefully by the teacher.

(1) *Purpose.*—The class members must see clearly the purpose of the field trip. They must feel a need which can be met by the trip. It is the task of the teacher, during a regular lesson period, to lead the class to become aware of a particular need and to point out the possibility of having this need met by a field trip.

(2) *Arrangements made.*—Certain arrangements must be made in advance. A place to be visited must be selected, the date and time set, and arrangements made for transportation and for a guide on the tour, if one is needed.

(3) *Proper background preparation.*—Although the class may understand the purpose for the trip, additional preparation is also necessary. This involves three things: First, the teacher will want to deepen the interest and heighten the motivation of the class for the trip. Second, he will need to orient them for the trip. The class should be given a general description of what they may expect to see. Third, they should be given specific guidance in what to look for. The class which just goes to look will miss some of the most important things they should have noted. This guidance may be provided by giving the class a list of questions to which they are to find answers on the trip. Or the teacher may let the members suggest what they would like to find out. Let them make a list. This list may then be sent to the proper person at the place to be visited so that, if possible, the members will have an opportunity to see that which answers their questions.

(4) *Take the trip.*—As the group takes the trip the teacher will call attention to matters he wants them to note. The members of the class will ask questions seeking to clarify some aspect they do not understand or to get more information. Thus the

process of analyzing, evaluating, and applying information takes place to some extent all during the trip.

(5) *Discussion after the trip.*—For learning purposes this is one of the most important of all the steps. An opportunity should be provided as soon after the trip as possible for the class members to discuss what they saw. Here they will raise other questions and have them answered. They will identify the insights gained and indicate the impressions felt.

(6) *Action to be taken.*—The class will decide on the action that ought to be taken. Of course if the trip was for the purpose of getting information, this step would be omitted.

(7) *Letter of appreciation.*—Following the trip a letter of appreciation to the place visited is always a courteous gesture. Such an expression makes the person who had the responsibility for arranging your visit feel that the effort given was worth while and makes him more willing for another group to come at another time.

Field trip opportunities.—A field trip may be as simple as visiting a church down the street or as elaborate as taking a trip out of town. The opportunities for learning experiences through field trips are almost limitless. In at least one state there is a plan for a field trip extending over several days during which the participants visit the various denominational institutions in the state. One seminary charters a bus twice each year to take students on a field trip to the denominational headquarters for a day-long tour. The average Sunday school teacher probably will not undertake such ambitious trips as these. Nevertheless there are numerous learning opportunities surrounding every church. The following are worth considering:

Visit a church of another faith
Visit a church of another denomination
Visit a needy area of the community
Visit a court while it is in session
Visit a jail
Visit the emergency room of a large hospital on Saturday night

Visit a denominational hospital
Visit a denominational college
Visit denominational headquarters
Visit a denominational children's home
Visit a home for the aged

Values of the field trip.—The field trip has an emotional appeal that can come only through a firsthand experience. It makes learning more real and more lasting because the learning comes through activity.

The field trip develops attitudes as well as giving factual information. So often attitudes are rather shallow and superficial because they are based on secondhand information. Christians speak glibly about the need for eliminating the liquor traffic. But a field trip to the emergency room of a city hospital on Saturday night may put so much deeper conviction into their attitudes through firsthand observation of the results of this evil that they will *do* something. Christians talk about their concern for the underprivileged in the community, but a trip to the slum area may put so much more meaning into this concern that they will *do* something about it.

Bulletin Board

The bulletin board in the Sunday school classroom is often used for announcements, posters, and other promotional materials. However, the concern here is for the use of the bulletin board as a teaching aid. Pictures, newspaper or magazine articles, and other items illustrating the lesson may be placed on the bulletin board. Each time the members look at the board they will be reminded of the truth that was discussed. This helps deepen learning. Class members should be encouraged to bring pictures and items of information related to the study being made.

At least three major principles should be kept in mind in using the bulletin board. First, the material posted should be related to the study being made. Second, the material on the board should be kept fresh and up-to-date. Third, the material should be attractively arranged.

Objects

An object may be described as the thing itself. Man's early learning came through a contact with things. He still learns in this way. Through the use of objects the teacher gives the class direct contact with things with which they may be unfamiliar. Since the class cannot go to lands where mission work is done, a part of the unfamiliar environment of these lands and people —clothing, coins, and household articles—may be brought to the class. One church has a museum of objects and articles brought by missionaries from other countries. The teachers may check these out for use when needed. Objects from Bible times may also be used effectively. A small, inexpensive Jewish Torah (scroll) can be purchased to show the class. A Palestinian lamp, coin, or other small articles make teaching much more realistic.

Models

A model may be described as a "replica of the thing itself." Today's children are familiar with models through their experience with them both in school and in their play. Hardly a boy has not at some time made a model airplane, car, or boat. Adults are familiar with models through their use in the armed services and in business training. Actually in many cases a model may be a more effective teaching aid than the actual thing itself.

This discussion has to do primarily with models that the class will make. As the members gather information needed to build a model, valuable learning takes place. For example, though Christians have studied about the Temple in Jerusalem all their lives, not many of them have a clear idea of what it looked like. The class might be led to make a model of the Temple showing the wailing wall, the Court of the Gentiles, the warning stones, the Court of the Women, the Court of Israel, the Court of the Priests, and the Temple proper, or sanctuary, which had two rooms. The class would learn more about the Temple in the process of studying to make a model than they would in almost any other way. The class might make a model of the city of Jerusalem, a model of a Palestinian house, and so on.

The model does not have to be a work of perfection unless the class wants to make it so. It is the learning that is important. Of course it takes time to make a model, but the enterprising teacher can help his members learn effectively with this aid. The models made should be kept for later use with other classes.

Charts

Charts are used to show relationship of persons, ideas, places, or things. They are used extensively and effectively in business and can be so used in Sunday school classes. The chart may be large for the whole class to see or it may be small for individual use. It may be placed on paper or poster board for more permanent use or it may be drawn on the chalkboard for temporary use. One class of Young Adults made a large chart of early Hebrew history showing outstanding persons, significant dates, and major events. For the first time this history began to make sense to them. A chart may be made of the Period of the Divided Kingdom showing the kings, the dates they ruled, and the major events. A "tree chart" may be made showing the family tree of Joseph. If a class has a quarter's lessons on "The Eighth Century Prophets," they may want to make a chart with columns, and as the study progresses fill in information showing the name of each prophet, the dates, the country in which his work was done, the king who was ruling, the social and spiritual condition of the country, and the essential message of the prophet. Such a chart would help the members see these events and their relation to other events clearly.

Graphs

A graph is a visual presentation of statistical or numerical data. Statistics given verbally are often meaningless and are soon forgotten. A visual presentation helps the class see relationships and comparisons more clearly. Graphs may be large or small; they may be drawn on paper, poster board, or chalkboard. Complete accuracy as to detail in the charts is not necessary to give the class the general idea desired. If the lesson is on the Cooperative Program, the teacher may use a pie chart (a circle divided into segments) to show the class the per cent that goes to each item. If the lesson is on stewardship, the teacher may want to use a chart showing the local church budget. Or if the lesson is on missions the teacher may use a bar graph showing the per cent of the local church budget used for local expenses and the amount set aside for missions. Instead of having the attendance record read aloud each Sunday a line graph in the classroom or department could show the attendance by Sundays over the past several years. A different color line could be used for different years. When statistics are needed, a visual presentation is almost a necessity.

Drama

Drama has been used widely in teaching small children, but those who teach older groups—even adults—have missed a real teaching opportunity by their failure to use drama. This is not to suggest that adults should be led to act out the story of the Good Samaritan. How, then, can drama be used with these groups?

Space does not permit a full discussion of this topic, but people of all ages enjoy participating in or watching a drama. Both participating and watching can be learning experiences. Role playing is a type of drama that can be engaged in during the class period. If the lesson is based on the verse "A soft answer turneth away wrath: but grievous words stir up anger" (Prov. 15:1), the teacher of a class for teen-agers might ask two members to role play this situation. One is quite angry and is trying to stir up trouble with the other. The other seeks to act like a Christian by giving a soft answer. After the situation has been acted out spontaneously for two or three minutes, the teacher might lead the class in considering the following questions: How did the person who was angry feel about the soft answers? How did the person giving the soft answers feel? Was the soft answer approach cowardly? Did it work?

A class of adults may be studying the book of Job for several Sundays. They may decide to write a drama of the book in modern language. As they study the book to write what each character is to say, they will learn more about the essential meaning of the book than they have ever known before.

Guidance in Lesson Preparation

The following questions will serve to guide the superintendent and teachers as they prepare the lesson they are to teach on Sunday.

1. Can the chalkboard be used in teaching this lesson?

2. If so, how will it be used?

(1) Outline lesson?

(2) Emphasize certain points?

(3) List ideas of the class?

(4) Other ways?

3. In what places in the lesson will the chalkboard be used?

4. Is there an occasion to use a map in this lesson?

5. For what purpose is it to be used? When and how is it to be used in the lesson plan?

6. Should the class be led to make a map to deepen their learning?

7. Will the use of flat pictures contribute to learning in this lesson?

8. How will they be used?

(1) To introduce the lesson?

(2) To illustrate a point?

(3) Other ways?

9. Should the class be led to take a field trip to deepen and enrich their learning?

10. What arrangements need to be made?

11. Can the bulletin board be used in teaching this lesson?

12. Will the use of objects make the teaching more realistic?

13. Should the class be led to make a model?

14. Will the use of a chart help the class to see historical relationships more clearly? Will the chart be of a permanent type (on paper or poster board) or will it simply be put on the chalkboard?

15. Will the use of a graph make statistics more meaningful?

16. Is there an opportunity to use drama?

13. Projected Visual Aids

THE EFFECTIVENESS OF PROJECTED VISUAL AIDS has been demonstrated beyond question in public schools, the armed services, and business. They are equally effective when used in the Sunday school. The four types which will be considered in this discussion are motion films, filmstrips, slides, and opaque projection.

Projected visual aids utilize certain basic principles of learning. First, learning is based upon interest. Projected aids, regardless of the type used, almost compel attention and interest on the part of the learner. The darkened room and the projected picture focus attention on what is being shown.

Second, learning is based on need. Often a person may be made more aware of a need in his personal life when a visual aid is used. Projected aids may also be used to lead class members to be keenly aware of needs in society or on a mission field. It is readily apparent how much more effective a visual presentation would be than a verbal presentation. Third, people learn through activity. Visual aids arouse and stimulate mental activity. Members more readily discuss what they have seen. They are often stimulated to action in the form of projects. Fourth, visual presentation aids in the problem of individual differences. All class members are not verbally minded. That is, they do not learn well through the use of words alone. Pictures provide the whole group with a common visual experience. While visual materials do not provide a firsthand experience, they do provide a secondhand experience which may be entered vicariously.

The Problem of Verbalism

Those who seek to teach religion are constantly plagued by the problem of verbalism. Actually there are two dangers involved in this one problem. First of all there is the danger that class members may learn words which have little or no meaning for them. When a teacher uses words as the primary means of teaching a Christian truth, there is always the possibility that the members may learn words without understanding the real or full meaning of those words. A recent article told of a small child who was learning to say the Lord's Prayer. Instead of saying, "Our Father which art in heaven, Hallowed be thy name," she said, "Our Father, which art in New Haven, how did you know my name?" Nor is this problem limited to small children. A group of adults will falter if they are asked the meaning of regeneration, justification, sanctification, and similar words.

There is a second danger which, if anything, is even more serious. When the teacher uses only words as the means of teaching a Christian ideal there is always the danger that the member may learn the words that describe the experience without actually experiencing the truth. Of course the teacher is concerned that the members learn the meaning of the words they use, but he also desires much more. He desires that the members *experience* the truths which the words describe. The use of visual aids can be an aid to overcoming this problem. A visual presentation of the truth in action helps the members to see more clearly the meaning of the truth in their own experience.

Projected visual aids help abstract ideas become more concrete. Christians are admonished to "bless them that curse you, do good to them that hate you, and pray for them which despitefully use you and persecute you." But how? What are some common experiences in life in which this truth may and should be expressed? Visual aids can help these truths become alive and concrete. Visual aids enable the learner to overcome the restrictions of limited personal experience. The personal experience of every individual is restricted by time. Yet a visual presentation can give him a reproduction of experiences that have happened in the past with which he may identify himself.

The learner's own experience is also limited by space. A visual presentation can bring to the learner these far away places, the people, their needs, and their problems. Finally, learning through direct, firsthand experience is limited by certain undesirable results that may attend these experiences. It would obviously be undesirable for young people to learn of the evils of alcoholism by firsthand experience. But a film can help the youth to see this evil clearly without having to experience it himself.

Visual aids help the learner to confront in a more realistic way personal and social problems. What does it mean to be a Christian witness? In what ways is the individual falling short? What does Christian stewardship mean? What are some pressing problems in society? What can be done about these problems? A visual presentation is a most effective aid in helping the learner develop or change an attitude. This is one of the objectives the Christian teacher most deeply desires. He wants to help his members develop those attitudes that are more Christian and express those attitudes in life. A visual aid presents a situation with emotional appeal. The learner tends to identify himself with persons and/or causes that appeal to him emotionally. Projected visual aids are powerful and effective tools which are available for the teacher to use in accomplishing his spiritual objectives. Surely he will want to take advantage of them.

Principles of Utilization

Visual aids, particularly motion films, have come to be identified in the minds of most people with entertainment. However, visual materials used in the Sunday school are not primarily for enjoyment but for learning. For this reason the teacher needs to understand clearly the difference between showing a film and *using* a film. For most effective learning there are certain principles of utilization that should be followed regardless of the type of projected visual aid used.[1] In using projected visual materials the teacher should understand and follow these steps without fail.

Purpose.—The purpose chosen by the teacher determines everything else that is done in the lesson. The purpose, of course, should be based on the Scripture passage being studied and the specific needs of the particular class.

Material.—Is there any visual material that deals with the lesson and the purpose the teacher has chosen? This may be a determining factor in the selection of the type of aid to be used.

Ordering.—If the material has to be ordered from the denominational book store or some other source, be sure to order well in advance. These materials are limited. The teacher will not be able to wait until the week the lesson is to be taught to decide to use a visual aid. If the teacher decides to use a filmstrip or slides, these materials may be found in the local church library.

Preview the material.—Previewing is an absolute essential. The teacher should preview the material, first of all, to become familiar with it himself. He will want to make sure that there are no objectional features. But most of all he needs to preview the material in order to determine how it is to be used and how it is to fit into the total lesson plan. Some filmstrip manuals contain the pictures from the strips to facilitate previewing.

Plan.—The teacher will plan how the visual material is to be introduced. Remember, the material is to be used, not just shown. This introduction should prepare the class for seeing the visual presentation and lead them to know what to look for.

The teacher will also plan proper questions for discussion after the film or other material is presented. In this follow-up discussion the teacher has the opportunity to guide the thinking of the class. What insights were gained? What problems

---

[1] Experiments indicate that when certain principles are followed (including proper introduction and follow-up) learning is increased up to 50 per cent.

were raised? Questions will be asked and answered; comments will be made; and perhaps decisions will be made. It is through this discussion that the teacher seeks to achieve his lesson objective. One cannot stress too strongly the importance of careful preparation here.

Equipment.—It is wise to set equipment up on Saturday whenever possible. Most people cannot or do not get to church early enough on Sunday morning to secure the equipment, set it up, and be assured of a smooth mechanical operation before the members begin to arrive. The electrical outlets should be checked and the room prepared for darkening and ventilation. The chairs should be properly arranged. Everything should be in complete readiness so there will be no distractions.

Introduction.—This introduction should fit into the teacher's total lesson plan. The teacher should indicate to the class the problem with which the material deals, stimulate the class to want to see the material, and raise some questions, the answers to which the class will find in the visual presentation.

Presentation.—Appropriate comments should be made and questions raised during the presentation if filmstrips, slides, or opaque projection is being used. There will be times when the teacher will not want (or need) to use an entire motion film. The teacher may also use only a part of a filmstrip that relates directly to the problem the class is considering. Thus the visual aid becomes an integral part of the lesson plan.

Follow-up discussion.—After the visual material has been presented, the teacher should lead the class to discuss what they saw. Comments will be made both by the teacher and the class members. Questions will be asked and answered, insights will be identified, and decisions will be made.

Motion Films

A brief consideration of the various types of projected visual aids will be helpful. The motion film is probably the most widely known, and for this reason it will be considered first.

Advantages.—Each aid has its own particular advantages and limitations. There is no one aid that is best for all occasions. As the teacher must select the method that will best achieve his desired objective, he must also select the particular visual aid that will best achieve his purpose.

(1) The motion film compels attention and secures interest. Probably no other visual aid is as effective as the motion film in this regard.

(2) It is particularly effective in those situations where meanings involve motion. There are certain situations where the class needs to see clearly the relationships of things, ideas, or events. For example, a motion film can picture most effectively the cause and effect of drinking upon broken homes.

(3) The illusion of motion makes for a sense of reality. When there is action on the screen, it makes the characters or the events become alive for the class. Paul, as a person, may become truly alive and the events that happened on his missionary journeys may become more meaningful to the class members as they see a film.

(4) Because of this sense of reality, the film touches the emotions. As the class sees the hunger of people in the world, orphans made homeless by war, evils and ills in society, emotions are touched. This is important in teaching, for emotions must be touched before action will take place.

Limitations.—The motion film, effective as it is, also has certain limitations.

(1) A very practical consideration is the expense involved. The cost of the motion film projector is considerably higher than other types of projectors. Also, the rental fee for films is sometimes high.

(2) The motion film projector is more complicated than other types. However, it is not really difficult to operate.

(3) It is not especially effective if motion or action is not essential in the situation being viewed. For example, if a teacher wants to help the class see the mountainous terrain of a coun-

try, a "still" picture is usually more practical than a motion film. Or, if the teacher wants to show the class the type of dress worn in a certain country or the type of house in which the people live, action is not essential, and information could better be secured through flat pictures, slides, or filmstrips.

(4) While the motion film is being shown the teacher tends to be relegated to the background. With the film's rapid-fire manner of projection, it is difficult if not impossible to have questions raised and answered or for the teacher to make any kind of comment or explanation. This would be true only while the film is actually being viewed. In introducing the film and in the follow-up the teacher still has a place of central importance.

(5) When a motion film is used, the mind-set of the class usually expects entertainment. For this reason the teacher must take special care in his introduction and follow-up discussion to help the group learn from the presentation.

Difficulties.—Although the motion film is an exceedingly effective aid in teaching, there are certain problems involved in using it in a Sunday school classroom. First, the bulkiness of the equipment makes it difficult to place in a small classroom. This would certainly be true in the small Junior and Intermediate classes and would also be true in the somewhat larger Adult classrooms. Second, the length of many films constitutes a problem. When the class teaching session is only thirty minutes, a film of this length would not give time for an adequate introduction or follow-up discussion. However, an increasing number of short films are now being produced, so this is becoming less of a problem.

Third, the price of film rentals presents a difficulty when used with a small group. The teacher might be hesitant, and with good cause, to pay eight or ten dollars to rent a film when it is to be seen by only eight to twelve people. Many churches are overcoming this problem by making multiple use of a given film. One group in Sunday school and another group in Training Union may use the same film for the same rental. However, until smaller and less expensive projectors are made and correspondingly less expensive materials are produced, the use of motion films will largely be limited to department assemblies and other large group meetings.

It is not recommended that classes be combined for the purpose of using films or that entire departments be shown a film using the class period teaching time. There may be exceptions, of course, but these should be rare.

Films in the department assembly.—Motion films are often used in the department assembly for purposes of worship. This is valuable, but films may be used in the department assembly for the purpose of teaching. In this way the motion film may be a most effective aid.[2] The film is used in the assembly period by the superintendent, and in the class period that follows each teacher uses the material presented in the film as the basis for discussion. This means that there must be close co-operation between the department superintendent and the teachers because the assembly period and the class period must be planned as one total teaching unit.

How is this planning to be done? The department superintendent and teachers will decide well in advance with which lesson a motion film is to be used. This should be done from four to six weeks ahead of time. This decision may be made at the time the teachers preview the lessons to be taught the next quarter. When the film arrives, the department superintendent and teachers should meet together to preview it. Having seen the picture, they will then determine together what their aim is to be and how the department superintendent can best introduce the film in the assembly. The follow-up discussion of the film will be done by each teacher in his classroom. The teachers

[2] The length of the film is an important factor when used in the department assembly. Since the assembly ought not to last over twenty minutes, the film used should not exceed thirteen minutes in length in order that a proper introduction can be made. A number of excellent films this length are available.

therefore plan together their teaching sessions, keeping in mind how the film is to be used in this discussion.

What are ways in which motion films may be used in the department assembly and then related to the lesson which follows?[3] Some suggestions are listed. Superintendents and teachers will think of others.

(1) To introduce a quarter's lessons.

(2) To review a quarter's lessons.

(3) To present a social problem.

(4) To make Bible material become alive.

(5) To introduce a study of missions.

(6) To introduce a Christian ideal such as stewardship or evangelism.

Filmstrips

Filmstrips may not have the glamour that motion pictures have, but in certain situations and for certain purposes they are even more effective teaching aids. Unlike motion films, filmstrips may be used by the teacher in the individual classrooms. The projectors are small, and the materials are sufficiently inexpensive to permit their use in the classroom. Teachers who are not now using this aid are overlooking an important means of making learning more interesting, more lasting, and more meaningful.[4]

Advantages.—So often when teachers think of projected visual aids, they think only of motion films. This is unfortunate because "still" projected aids have their own particular advantages. What are some advantages of filmstrips?

(1) There is a wealth of material available. More educational material is available in this form at the present time than any

---

[3] *Focus,* a denominational audio-visual catalogue, contains a listing and brief description of films and filmstrips which are available. It also gives a listing of slides and slide sets. This catalogue may be obtained by writing a Baptist Book Store.

[4] There is an excellent filmstrip entitled, "Using Filmstrips in the Church," which could be used with the teachers in studying this topic.

other. Whether the teacher desires visual material to help teach the Bible, to deal with the Christian home, youth problems, or some other area, he is likely to find a filmstrip dealing with the topic. This is an advantage of no small significance.

(2) This aid is relatively inexpensive. The projector does not cost nearly as much as the motion film projector, and almost any church can afford to own one or more of these projectors. The filmstrips themselves are likewise inexpensive. They should be purchased by the church and kept in the church library for use with different groups from year to year.

(3) A third advantage when the church purchases these filmstrips is they are available when needed by the teacher. The teacher does not have to write to a film library in order to secure the material.

(4) The equipment is quite simple to operate. Most teachers who are unfamiliar with projectors are frightened by the thought of trying to use this mechanical device. The filmstrip and slide projector is so simple the teacher can learn to operate it in a very short time.

(5) Since the filmstrip is in a fixed sequence the pictures do not get out of place as slides sometimes do.

(6) Since each frame of the filmstrip can be left on the screen for a long period of time, the teacher has an opportunity to make necessary explanations and to ask and answer questions during the showing. This makes for a much more effective teaching situation.

Limitations.—However, the filmstrip, like every other visual aid, has its limitations.

(1) Obviously it is not as effective in those situations where motion or action is essential.

(2) It usually does not have the emotional appeal that motion films have.

(3) Being in a fixed sequence, the pictures cannot be rearranged to fit a particular need the teacher might have in presenting a certain lesson.

(4) Time and effort are required to set up the equipment. But of course it takes some time and effort for the teacher to plan the lesson regardless of the method to be employed in teaching.

Using the filmstrip.[5]—When the teacher plans to use a filmstrip, he must observe the principles of utilization that were discussed earlier in the chapter. He must have a clear aim in mind. He must select the filmstrip related to that aim and plan to use it as a part of his total lesson plan. He must plan how it is to be introduced, and how the follow-up discussion is to be led. Since he will do the talking while the strip is being viewed, he also must plan what he is to say, what he is to point out, and what questions he might ask.

The filmstrip is one of the best means available for giving information. Does the class need information about Bible backgrounds, about one of the characters or events in the Old Testament, about the life and ministry of Jesus, about Paul, about the customs and dress of Bible times, about the geography of Palestine? Use a filmstrip to make this information vivid to the class members. A filmstrip may be used also to introduce or to preview a quarter's lessons. Does the lesson deal with some so-

---

[5] Filmstrips also can be used with great effectiveness in leadership education in the local church. (1) In the area of teacher training there is the Teaching Improvement Series. This is a series of five filmstrips: "The Christian Teacher," "Selecting Aims," "Choosing Methods," "Planning a Lesson," "Testing Results." (2) In the area of age group studies there is the Age Group Series: "Cradle Roll Sunday School Work," "Providing for Nursery Children," "Guiding Nursery Children," "Beginner Sunday School Work," "Primary Sunday School Work," "Junior Sunday School Work," "Intermediate Sunday School Work," "Young People's Sunday School Work," "Adult Sunday School Work," "Extension Department Sunday School Work." (3) In the area of training Sunday school class officers there is the Class Officer Series: "Class Officers At Work," "Sunday School Class President," "Sunday School Class Vice-President," "Sunday School Class Group Leaders," "Sunday School Class Secretary." (4) In the area of general leadership training there are other excellent filmstrips: "The Weekly Officers and Teachers' Meeting," "An Adequate Training Program," "Associational Sunday School Work," "How To Have a Vacation Bible School," "Laws of Sunday School Growth," "Using Records Effectively," "Ye Visited Me." There are also filmstrips dealing with Training Union work: "The Training Union Executive Committee" and "Training Union Officers' Council."

cial problem such as juvenile delinquency, or with a personal problem such as boy-girl relations, or with some Christian ideal, or with missions? Filmstrips are available to help the teacher with his teaching.

Slides

Slides have been used often as an aid to worship in department assemblies, but the use of slides as aids to teaching in the classroom will be considered here. What are some of the advantages of this aid to teaching?

Advantages.—

(1) The projector is small enough to be used in the classroom. It is light enough to be carried easily. It is quite easy to operate.[6]

(2) Slides can be used in direct relation to what is being taught in the lesson. The teacher may need to use a slide in the introduction. Later in the lesson a slide may be used to give information about a point being discussed. Slides may be used all at one time, or they may be interspersed throughout the lesson.

(3) There is a wealth of educational material available.

(4) When slides are purchased by a church and placed in the church library, they can be used by many different groups for many different purposes. A slide may be used with one group on one Sunday to help teach the life of Jesus. The same slide may be used in a different class on another Sunday to show what a Palestinian house looks like. The same slide may be used still another Sunday with still another group to show the dress, the customs, or the life in Palestine.

(5) They can be used in a semidark room. Complete darkness is not required.

---

[6] It is recommended that a church purchase a combination slide-filmstrip projector rather than a separate slide projector and filmstrip projector. If sufficient funds are available to purchase two projectors, purchase two combination slide-filmstrip projectors.

(6) A slide can be left on the screen indefinitely, permitting careful study and questions by the class plus comments and questions by the teacher.

(7) Slides have a flexibility that is unsurpassed. The teacher may choose to use only a few from the set. Another teacher may decide that he wants to use the slides in a different order on another Sunday because his lesson purpose is different from the first teacher's.

Limitations.—As with all types of projected visual aids, slides have certain limitations. It takes some time and effort to set up the equipment. The mechanical details must be cared for in advance. Like filmstrips, slides are not particularly effective in situations where motion is essential to meaning. A slide may be projected upside-down if care is not exercised, causing an unwanted interruption to the teaching of the lesson.

Uses of the slide.—Slides have much the same uses as filmstrips. They can be used to introduce or review a single lesson or quarter's lessons. They are excellent for teaching about life in Bible times or life on the mission field. They can be used to introduce a problem for discussion.

Many people are now making their own slides. Teachers may do this and make their teaching much more personal. For example, if the lesson is on missions, and if the aim of the teacher is to stimulate interest in starting a mission in a needy area of the community, he can take a series of slides of the area and use them in his class to make the awareness of the need more real.

Opaque Projection

Opaque projection is probably the least well known of all the projected aids, yet it can be used with great profit. It uses reflected light and a set of mirrors to project a flat picture on the screen.

Advantages.—What are some advantages of this teaching aid?

(1) Materials to be used are always at the teacher's finger-tips. Pictures to be used may be found in books, magazines, denominational periodicals, or newspapers. A book may be placed in the projector and a picture or paragraph shown to the class. Pictures may be shown whether mounted or unmounted. The availability of material is limited only by the resourcefulness of the teacher.

(2) Pictures can be easily mounted and stored for repeated use.

(3) The picture appears on the screen in its natural color. The quality of the color is limited only by the color in the picture.

(4) The projector is quite versatile. It can be used for a variety of purposes and can be cut on and off as needed in the teaching situation.

(5) It is very simple to operate.

Limitations.—

(1) The machine is bulky and heavy to carry around.

(2) The projector costs about twice as much as slide-film-strip projectors.

(3) It is limited in the size of the picture it can project. Most opaque projectors can take pictures only up to 10 inches by 10 inches in size.

(4) Perhaps the most serious limitation is the fact that almost total darkness in the room is needed to give good viewing. Because it uses reflected light, it is not strong enough to use in semidark rooms.

Guidance In Lesson Preparation

It is highly important that the department superintendent plan well in advance when this topic is to be used with his teachers. First, he should plan to use it on a Wednesday night when the lesson for the following Sunday lends itself to the use of a projected aid. Second, he should plan sufficiently in advance so that the projected aid (particularly if it is a motion film) can be ordered and will be available for use by the teachers on the desired Sunday. As the teachers preview the lessons for the quarter, they can decide which Sunday or Sundays they desire to use projected aids. Third, he should use some visual aid as he presents this topic to the teachers. He should do more than lecture on the value of visual aids.

1. The teachers will determine the aim of the lesson.

2. In light of the lesson aim decide which projected aid can best accomplish this objective. (Actually, these two steps should have been done in advance by the superintendent and teachers so that the desired material will be available.)

3. Make sure that the visual material selected is related to and will contribute to achieving the lesson purpose.

4. Review with the teachers the principles of utilization. These must be followed for most effective results.

5. Is a motion film to be used in the department assembly period? If so, this means that the department superintendent and the teachers must plan the total session together.

(1) Preview the film together.

(2) How will the superintendent introduce the film?

(3) How will the teachers use the film in the classroom?

6. Is a filmstrip to be used?

(1) How will it fit into the total lesson plan?

(2) Be sure to review and observe the principles of utilization.

(3) What comments will be made during the viewing of the filmstrip?

(4) What questions will be asked?

7. Are slides to be used?

(1) For what purpose are they to be used?

(2) How will they be used in the lesson plan?

8. Will opaque projection be used?

(1) Have the desired pictures been secured?

(2) Should they be mounted?

(3) How will they be used in the lesson plan?

The Library of Congress has catalogued this book as follows:

Edge, Findley Bartow, 1916– . Helping the teacher.
  Nashville, Broadman Press [1959] 181 p. 21 cm. 1.
  Religious education—Teaching methods. 2. Sunday-
  schools. i. Title. BV1534.E33 (268.6) 59–5854

Edge, Findley B.

Helping the teacher

HB $2.95

Edge, Findley B.

Helping the teacher

HB $2.95

DATE	ISSUED TO